#FEARHUNTERS

*HOW TO REMOVE THE FEAR AND SHAME
THAT STAND BETWEEN YOU AND
THE LIFE YOU ARE DESTINED TO LIVE*

NOAH ELIAS

FOREWORD BY BOB SHANK

#Fearhunters
Copyright 2018 Noah Elias

Unless otherwise noted, all Scripture taken from the NEW AMERICAN
STANDARD BIBLE®, Copyright © 1960, 1962, 1963, 1968, 1971, 1972, 1973, 1975,
1977, 1995 by The Lockman Foundation. Used by permission.

Scriptures marked KJV are taken from the KING JAMES VERSION (KJV): KING
JAMES VERSION, public domain.

The ESV® Bible (The Holy Bible, English Standard Version®). ESV® Permanent
Text Edition® (2016). Copyright © 2001 by Crossway, a publishing ministry of
Good News Publishers. The ESV® text has been reproduced in cooperation with
and by permission of Good News Publishers. Unauthorized reproduction of this
publication is prohibited. All rights reserved.

THE HOLY BIBLE, NEW INTERNATIONAL VERSION®, NIV® Copyright ©
1973, 1978, 1984, 2011 by Biblica, Inc.® Used by permission. All rights reserved
worldwide.

Scripture taken from The Message. Copyright © 1993, 1994, 1995, 1996, 2000,
2001, 2002. Used by permission of NavPress Publishing Group.

Scripture marked (BSB) taken from The Holy Bible, Berean Study Bible, BSB
Copyright ©2016 by Bible Hub
Used by Permission. All Rights Reserved Worldwide.

Scripture quotations marked (NLT) are taken from the Holy Bible,
New Living Translation, copyright © 1996, 2004, 2007 by
Tyndale House Foundation. Used by permission of Tyndale House
Publishers, Inc., Carol Stream, Illinois 60188. All rights reserved.

Scripture quotations marked NKJV from the New King James Version. Copyright
© 1982 by Thomas Nelson, Inc. Used by permission. All rights reserved.

Cover Design by Human
Interior Design by Renee Evans
Produced by Noah Fine Art:
www.noah neart.com

Hardcover ISBN: 978-1-942306-81-8
Paperback ISBN: 978-1-947165-66-3

Printed in the United States

#DEDICATION

I'd like to dedicate this book to Chantel for being with me as I entered the pit to rescue my true self. Your support and unconditional love have been invaluable. Thank you to Noah and Griffin for showing me what joy means and what fun looks like.

Lastly, to my mentors Bob Shank and Dave Carder, you have been my wingmen through the darkest seasons but revealed the truth that set me free.

#CONTENTS

FOREWORD - 1

INTRODUCTION - 5

PART ONE
UNDERSTAND THE BATTLE AND GEAR UP FOR THE FIGHT

CHAPTER 1:   Living the Perfect Nightmare - 13

CHAPTER 2:   The Problem and the Goal - 21

CHAPTER 3:   Defining the Enemy: What Is Fear? What Is
            Shame? - 29

CHAPTER 4:   The Enemy's Co-conspirator: The False Self - 39

CHAPTER 5:   How Does the Enemy Fight? - 45

CHAPTER 6:   Counterattack: Fear-Based Symptoms
            Debunked - 57

CHAPTER 7:   Enemy Battleground: The Power of Choice - 81

PART TWO
ENTER THE PIT: VISIT THE NIGHTMARE, RESCUE THE CHILD WITHIN, AND DEFEAT THE ENEMY

CHAPTER 8:   A Radical New Life: Become a Fearhunter - 93
CHAPTER 9:   Love: The Heart of the Matter - 101
CHAPTER 10: Mental Hoarding: Holding on to Lies and
                       False Self-Identities - 109
CHAPTER 11: The Shame Game - 121
CHAPTER 12: Disarming Bombs Through Compassion - 129

PART THREE
WALKING OUT OF THE MENTAL PRISON: STEPPING INTO FREEDOM, AUTHORITY, AND LIVING IN YOUR CALLING

CHAPTER 13: Discover Your Strengths - 149
CHAPTER 14: The Difference Between a Calling and
                       a Career - 165
CHAPTER 15: Becoming a Professional Failure - 173
CHAPTER 16: Aiming for Significance - 183
CHAPTER 17: Decisive Victory: Your True Authentic Self - 203
CHAPTER 18: Preventative Maintenance for Active Duty - 209
CHAPTER 19: Responding with Gratitude - 225
CHAPTER 20: Unconditional Surrender - 247

NOTES - 257
ADDITIONAL ACKNOWLEDGMENTS - 263
ABOUT THE AUTHOR - 265

FOREWORD

Every two years, the world becomes a captive audience to a global spectacle that commands the attention of people across every country around the world—the Olympics, staged in a host city that has spent millions in preparation for the event(s).

As I write, the Rio Olympics are still on the minds of the people who inserted into their summertime work or vacation schedules the television coverage of over 10,000 athletes who came together to deliver the performance of a lifetime.

A study of the men and women preparing to engage their specialty event would have been a graduate-level research effort. Emotions were on display on faces of every color as the seconds/minutes/hours they had sacrificed and trained for became their next life experience. By then, the physical comparability between the people in the lanes was far less an issue than the mindset they had as they made demands of their body that mere mortals—the spectators—would never imagine. What words could you use to describe the feelings of these world-class champions who were prepared to bring glory to their countries, their families, and themselves?

From that incredible and impressive field of competitors, there was one man who was—perhaps—the star of the show. His three gold medals were impressive, but it was the manner in which Usain Bolt won the 100 meters, 200 meters, and anchored the Jamaican team in the 4 x 100 meters relay. His face became the face of the 2016 Summer Olympic Games.

As the cameras zoomed in on Bolt as he prepared to run, there was no mistaking his emotional status: if you could carve joy into a statue, you would do no better than to choose Usain Bolt as your model. The contrast between his demeanor and that of the men in the other lanes was dramatic: he was loving life, from the crack of the starter pistol to the roar of the crowd as he crossed the finish lines, first.

Imagine the same scene with one shocking difference: Bolt, suited up to compete, but wearing a backpack stuffed with rocks. Add 40 pounds to his 207 pound frame: would that be enough to change the outcome of those races?

Only a fool would add an unnecessary ounce to an Olympic sprinter's starting-block form: in fact, every item of clothing is selected considering the delicate balance between weight and function. Streamlined is best, encumbered is unthinkable. If you're going for the gold, you offload the unnecessary.

In *#Fearhunters*, Noah Elias writes to people who have the potential to win—and win big—but who run the risk of missing the medal because of the rocks in their pack. What seems too obvious to an athlete on the track can be lost in the fog of life's course as men and women concede defeat to the weights that make their shoulders sag and their joy disappear.

What is holding you back from the front of the field? For most people, fear and shame are the biggies. Like boulders in a backpack, they are insidious additions that ensure defeat.

Fear is a parasite that sucks the potential out of the future; shame is a virus that we pick up from our past and don't know how to eliminate. Together, they represent enough compromise of one's health and vitality, making it impossible to deliver the world-class performance we long to deliver every day.

In Rio, the difference between wannabes and winners wasn't apparent. Often, it was the coaches who helped men and women with potential become athletes with medals and endorsements. Wisdom and objectivity—offered by someone who had earned trust with their own story—made the difference between achievement and almost. Where can you find that kind of input to take you from maybe to maturity?

Hire Noah to coach you; he's available at a bargain rate: the cost of this book and the time you'll devote to reading, considering, and incorporating his observations about the things that we are all likely to accumulate while living in the toxic environment that surrounds the stadium of life. The question is not, can you afford it? The real question is, *can you afford not to?*

The space between victory and defeat is usually inches—or seconds—and the gap is often closed by what's going on in the head and heart, not the arms and legs. Are you ready to make the moves—and come to the conclusions—that may send you home with the gold?

Find a quiet place to engage the *#Fearhunters* conversation and get ready to free yourself for a future that is more powerful than you've ever imagined possible.

Bob Shank

INTRODUCTION

Ever since childhood, I've had a nagging feeling that is like a constant hum or frequency in my head broadcasting fear, guilt, and shame. I didn't know what it was at the time, but the best way to describe it is fear self-talk. These fears took on many voices and many forms. Whether the external pressure came from kids on the playground, teammates, teachers, coaches, or any authority, I felt like I wasn't measuring up. I believe it is very important to hear verbal encouragement while growing up, yet it wasn't very often I would have someone tell me, "Hey kid, you have what it takes." I would often fear that something bad was about to happen. I had anxiety for no reason because I lived with the belief that I wasn't good enough. I never felt safe. As I look over the history of my life, I don't recall many times of peace or seasons of solace in my soul.

Fear and shame unknowingly became my friends because I didn't feel normal unless they were present. I turned to them because I became so used to functioning out of a place of fear that it felt familiar, and familiar is comfortable. I think we all experience turning to false identities for coping mechanisms to a certain extent. We choose false identities because it's easier than facing pain and discomfort. We give lies permission to rule our thinking. The problem is that the lies that fear and shame tell us can grow to a point of controlling our minds. Further, we believe the lies we tell ourselves, and it changes how we behave and the choices we make.

I grew up in a religious house and was part of the religious culture of youth groups and church on the weekends. My life focus was to avoid things that I wasn't supposed to do rather than embrace the good things that I should be doing. This religious culture was based on fear and shame. I remember hearing about love, joy, peace, patience, and kindness, but I didn't experience them in my own life. They were talked about a lot, but I didn't experience them personally with God. I felt as if I was forcing my way through.

This toxic culture created emotional wounds that began to grow. Unhealed emotional wounds infect our souls and spread. My anxiety and fear grew into my adult years because I let these wounds from my youth fester. What's more, as I grew up, I became a leader in my profession and craft, and the stakes got higher. Life became super intense the more I gravitated toward living my true self, meaning, as I drew closer to discovering my calling and taking bigger risks, fear, shame, and guilt showed up with a vengeance to try and shut me down.

Many of us live life on a hamster wheel, trying to control self-talk and second guessing every decision we make. We fear confrontation and indulge the self-hate that keeps us from expressing our true selves. We see advertisements on TV and in magazines that promote a life of peace and happiness. We scroll through Instagram, Facebook, and Pinterest to vicariously live the lives of others as they seemingly live in harmony with their kids, spouses, and community. Our mental capacity in this digital age has become redlined, and we numb ourselves with false identities—drugs, sex, food, work, and anything to keep from discovering our true self— all the while missing the present life. We aren't living; we are existing. The story in our heads is a life of management, not one of thriving in action.

It has only been in my adult life, through amazing friends and leaders who specialize in shame and fear, that I gained freedom from these feelings. I wrote this book to help others free themselves from these haunting feelings. People spend countless hours in counseling and thousands of dollars on medication to maintain or cope with an enemy that I believe can be eliminated and disposed of. The key is in "knowing" the truth and taking action in light of that truth. This book is meant to be your personal trainer and guide for the journey of eliminating fear and shame. Your job is to trust and repeat the process until you experience freedom. After this, it becomes routine maintenance.

This book is a collection of techniques, tools, and strategies that I've acquired over the years to remove the fears and shame that paralyzed me and kept me from the life I was created to live. I believe everyone desires the feeling of waking up each day knowing who they are, what they are supposed to do, and how they are supposed to do it. With this confidence comes peace of mind, and more importantly, it also comes with a life of hitting the bull's-eye of purpose and enables you to help others as well.

I am going to show you how to stop living where you are spread too thin, exhausted, and afraid of life. I am going to show you how to clear your heart and mind to make room for peace, love, and compassion for yourself. I am going to define the enemy and show you who and what you've been fighting, and how to go on the offense to hunt. We are not going on the hunt to simply wound or silence fear and shame —we are going in for the kill. When these thoughts, lies, and beliefs are removed, the incessant management of mental chaos decreases, and we regain the capacity for true authentic living and thriving in our true identities.

Once you have the noise of chaos management removed from your mind, we will dive into what it means to move into your authority. We discuss how to set up boundaries and guidelines for life that best suit your unique strengths so that you can experience the joy of doing what you were made to do. As this journey continues and you begin to move in your calling, we develop the bigger picture of stewarding your resources of time, money, and talent to help bring into focus a life of purpose and significance, rather than simply living for "success."

When you work out to build muscle, it takes time to see results. The great thing about your thoughts is that they can change immediately—the instant you practice these strategies and truths, you can start to see results. You can change today, this moment. You can get free, and 99 percent of getting free is *knowing* the truth. We often believe the lies and false identities about ourselves because we don't know the truth. Will you unlock the shackles and the gate of your own prison to run your own life? Or will you choose to remain inactive and trapped out of fear of the unknown?

INTRODUCTION

It is funny how mortals always picture us as putting things into their minds: in reality our best work is done by keeping things out.[1]

C. S. LEWIS, *THE SCREWTAPE LETTERS*

Why the title, *#Fearhunters*? When I went through my life transformation and healing, I wanted to help others achieve these same results. It was a difficult process to define with a name, so I dove into what the process *felt* like. The best way I could describe this process was going on the hunt for the toxic emotions that stood in the way of authentic living. I wanted to hunt down anything that caused me to retreat. Most people are terrified of facing confrontation, failure, relationships, and their true selves. I wanted to challenge this mindset of avoidance and go after the very thing that terrifies us the most. Imagine yourself not having to deal with what you've been carrying for so long. Imagine all of the baggage you've been tolerating for years—the baggage that seems to keep growing more powerful—disappearing. How does it sound to know, define, and get rid of these false identities so that you can have a positive impact on the world and do so from a place of rest?

You shall know the truth, and the truth shall make you free.

JESUS OF NAZARETH (JOHN 8:32, NKJV)

Hunting fear and shame isn't clean. It's messy, emotional, and in its truest form, spiritual. Life doesn't have to run us. We contain the most powerful weapons within ourselves. We just have to harness them and put them to use. When we do, it opens up a life that we never imagined.

9

I wrote this book with the intention to be as true to myself as I could. I wrote it based on what needed to be said and that's it. This might not be exactly the format you are used to, but I didn't want it to be cookie-cutter. This book is my raw strategy to get you to freedom as quickly and as simply as possible. Put that war paint on—we are going hunting.

PART ONE

UNDERSTAND THE BATTLE
AND GEAR UP FOR THE FIGHT

#CHAPTER 1

LIVING THE PERFECT NIGHTMARE

The worst nightmares and wounds from our past hold keys to unlocking our true identity and authentic self. Freedom lies in visiting and healing the child within.

NOAH

I WAKE UP JUST ENOUGH TO SQUINT MY EYES AS I REALIZE that I'm soaked in sweat. It's 4 a.m. I am a 40-year-old, happily married man with two beautiful children, and the owner of a few amazing companies. Externally, my world looks perfect to most people, and yet tonight, my heart is pounding at a rate that isn't normal for someone simply lying in bed. I am filled with dread as my mind is bombarded with a visual slide show playing out negative scenarios of everything I hold dear. Pictures of our children's futures and general well-being flash before my eyes. I envision negative outcomes of my businesses and question the validity of my efforts as a husband, father, and friend. These impressions inundate my mind like a flock of vultures on a fresh carcass. I sit up slightly in order to get my bearing, considering that it may be a nightmare. I run inventory in my head, questioning if any of these fears are true, and I find subtle relief in realizing that they are false. However, it takes time for my heart to find rest. I lay my head down and notice myself uttering praise and quoting Scripture, wondering if my wife, Chantel, can hear me going through this routine. I tell myself affirmations and pray against fear and shame and the onslaught of dark thoughts. I feel adrift in an ocean of terror, each wave submerging me just as I gasp for air. I attempt sleep in hopes that it's the last wave, and I mentally prepare for the worst. Physically and emotionally exhausted, I lay back down and eventually fall asleep. This experience makes me feel like a child, like an orphan alone in search of a hiding place. And I feel this way as a grown man with a seemingly perfect life.

I began building my business at a young age, one client and customer at a time. I was driven to have the perfect American life, and my career slowly began to take off. I was working with celebrities, painting portraits and murals, and building high-profile working relationships with large corporations such as Lexus, Levi Strauss, CBS Television, and others. Each relationship began a new opportunity and expansion of my journey. I had created custom designs for Universal Pictures featured in the major motion picture *2 Fast 2 Furious*, and was also featured on the MTV shows *Rob and Big*, and *Meet the Barkers*. One of my favorite and most fruitful partnerships has been with Disney, where I also developed distribution relationships with major outlets like Costco for this unique venture. It seemed I had the dream life and that everything was wonderful; however, along this journey I encountered fear like I had never known previously. Building and operating a business prompted so many fear-based obstacles that I had to confront and overcome. Whether it was negotiating a contract or dialoguing with vendors and accountants, I had to learn how to face these fears on my own.

It was 4 p.m. on a sunny Southern California afternoon. I was on my way to a very important meeting with one of my biggest clients. I was sitting in traffic near Burbank on Interstate 5 listening to classical music and enjoying the solitude when suddenly I felt a wave of anxiety and panic overtake me. I told myself, "Noah, everything is fine; there is no threat. Things are peaceful, and you're just sitting in traffic." The feeling was one of impending doom. I felt as if I were about to faint, and even thought I might die. It was horrible. I had no idea why this was happening. The moment lasted about eight seconds but felt like an eternity. My mind was racing: Am I coherent enough to safely pull over? How would they get a hold of my wife? Then I began to ask the bigger questions: What is wrong with me? Where are these events coming from? I knew that I couldn't keep living like this—I felt like I was on the verge of a breakdown and was barely containing these events. I needed to get to the root of these issues.

Fear, anxiety, and shame took root early in my life and grew into the monster that I have been describing. It's easy to look at people's highlight reel on social media and through the lens of their perfectly crafted marketing without knowing any backstory or understanding the sometimes dark underbelly of what they went through to get there. My life was messy, warped, and confusing before it became balanced, focused, and strategic. I remember being so emotionally sick that I wondered if life could get beyond mere survival. I wanted solace for my life, but I didn't understand how to express or receive compassion for myself, let alone anyone else. I didn't want to take this toxic shame and fear into my marriage, parenting, or career. I wanted it gone. Removed. Out of my life forever.

I had come to realize that the source of this mess began with one specific event and grew from there. My parents divorced when I was nine years old, forcing my sister and me to decide between living in Northern California with my dad or in Southern California with my mom. This altered the rest of my childhood and early development, as the fallout from divorce had consequences that I never would have imagined. I went to live with my grandparents during this transition and had to be transferred to a new school. I remember one scenario where I was sitting on the ground with the whole class while the teacher was reading a story at the front of the room. I began to weep. The teacher stopped and asked what was wrong and all the other kids looked at me. I just kept weeping. I don't remember how that morning turned out; I only remember experiencing the fear. This was one of many moments throughout my childhood and teenage years that I would later have to reconcile.

The trauma of my family being torn apart put me into a tailspin of distress. The trepidation I felt was a result of the uncertainty these events had caused that put our survival and security into question. I wasn't sure if either my mom or my dad were going to be OK, and I personally felt like I was in a continual state of fight or flight. Unpredictable people and situations became threats to my well-being, resulting in toxic thought patterns that began to be the norm of my daily life. This was the first time I experienced feeling like an orphan.

I coped with these feelings of uncertainty and dread by keeping myself busy. I hoped to drown out the noise inside my mind through productivity and interpreted success as security. I was compelled to build a business from a young age and had developed a passion for drawing, sign painting, and graphic design by the time I was 16. Computers weren't widespread by this time, so I would ride my bike door to door selling my art throughout Corona del Mar, California, and began to steadily generate income making art after school. Around the same time, I also had the option of pursuing a career in professional football, and I was touring with my rock band. I saw high school graduation as my pathway to freedom and to finally being able to step out into my own full-time journey. I was proud of my accomplishments, and it was helpful to stay busy; but the longer I buried these unresolved feelings, I would later realize, the more they grew.

Through prayer, introspection, and mentorship, I saw that these issues of fear, shame, and anxiety arose out of the turmoil from my childhood. I began digging to get to the root of the problem. I became a fearhunter. Undealt with, these toxic emotions manifest differently in each person, but there is a very real potential that it can stunt your growth and also hinder your destiny; they can enable a false identity designed to protect you from the things you fear, but also keep you from taking the risks required to step into your true identity. When this revelation hit me, I realized that part of my destiny is to release others from these traps. I immediately began looking for opportunities to liberate others from this oppression with the tools that I had learned. Fear, shame, and anxiety became such a preoccupation and hindrance in my life that I was forced to take action to remove them, and I wanted to see if the same process I used worked for other people as well as it did for me.

I remember mentoring a buddy of mine. (I have renamed him Jim for this book.) Jim was terrified of the job he was about to leave. I invited him to sit with me as I mapped out his life on whiteboards in my studio. I wanted him to literally see the facts of his fear and what he was imagining to be real. Most importantly, I wanted him to see his ideal, true self—the man he wanted to be. An amazing thing happens when we put pen to paper and visually see what we want to be, where we want to be, and what we want life to look like.

As I worked with him, I listed the biggest fears that he imagined, the fears that were going to keep him from making the decision to leave his job and step into the lifestyle and career where he created his own path. I asked him to identify the worst-case scenario that could occur as a result of making these decisions. I then had him make a wish list of dreams he would want to experience if he were living as his true self. Next, we drilled down to *why* he wanted them. Over the course of one day, his entire life changed. His mind was rewritten. He realized that the regret of living in indifference would suffocate him, and he would become a ghost of a husband, a dad, and man in his community. It would cost him more to stay where he was than it would to quit his job and pursue his ideal life.

After we had dismantled the false evidence that was weighing him down, Jim immediately started acting on these newfound beliefs and truths. He moved in action toward his true self and stopped wasting energy on maintaining his false life. He became a fearhunter. He started going on the hunt for the things that stood in the way of his authentic self. Jim is now on the offense.

This vital process had been started in Jim's life, and he set out to step into his ideal life and calling. The tools outlined in this book have worked to set me free, and I was so excited that I began helping others like Jim find freedom as well. I absolutely believe that if you take this journey with us, we will find your freedom too!

#CHAPTER 2

THE PROBLEM AND THE GOAL

One of the highest truths that I have discovered is that fear is the gateway between us and the destiny of who we are created to be. The fullness of our personality, creativity, and desires exist beyond this gateway of fear. The foundation of this door is built on the self-judgment that shrouds us in hiddenness. No matter how much I am loved or hated by those outside of me, I am the gatekeeper that peddles unlovable lies or deals lovable truth to this child within and keeps him trapped through my judgment or sets him free through my acceptance.[2]

JUSTIN STUMVOLL

If we don't live a true and authentic life, we are doing a disservice to God and our fellow man.

NOAH

YOU STAND IN AN EMPTY ROOM, BUT YOU ARE NOT TRULY alone. You are haunted by the presence of the ideal self. You see this person across the room and treat him or her like a glamorized avatar of the ideal *you*. You try to live with the idea that you are who you are now, but you constantly hope to be someone else, and you compare yourself to an ideal self in your mind.

So why don't you ask yourself, "What stands in the way of who I am now and who I want to be? Who is keeping me from living the life I have always wanted? What do I *fear* would happen if I pulled the trigger on living as the true, authentic me?"

THE PROBLEM TO SOLVE

As I see it, there are obstacles in our way keeping us from the life we want to live. The two main culprits for a stagnant life are fear and shame. Let's spend some time diagnosing fear and what it really is.

Fear and shame are feelings. Once you embrace this concept, it helps minimize their power over you. Fear and shame are false. They aren't reality, but they have probably been running your life in more areas and for longer than you think. Fear and shame are subtle, powerful misbeliefs that we allow to build up. They create a dialogue, which becomes a false identity that grows more powerful over time. This combo typically feels like not being good enough, not being valuable, not being seen, heard, or accepted. Basically, if I do X, it's going to mean people are disappointed in me and I am going to lose connection, acceptance, and nurturance. If I act as the real me, it will mean exposure for who I really am. Others might not accept me and then I will lose what I have. Let's face it. Nobody wants rejection or loss.

The doubts created by fear and shame start in our youth and become louder and louder as we navigate life. When we leave doubts unresolved, they fester. The more time goes on, the worse they get until we are faced with a brutal reality of time hunting us down. Time is the sober reminder that our life on earth is a gift, and we can either be fruitful or flatlined. We can either be a human being or simply a human existing. Additionally, we cannot allow our past memories to be greater than our future. We can't live in reverse. I've met a lot of individuals who claim, "The older I get, the better I was." Their "best" self or identity is a past memory as the cheerleader, football player, or something else in the glory days of high school.

As we reach adulthood, we are faced with a mountain of responsibility. We feel the pressure to grow up, get a career, start a family, and grab all the material security we can and coast our way to retirement and death. We hope that we can be good enough to hopefully escape to heaven someday. Is that really life? Good grief! There has got to be way more to it than that!

We need to recognize, define, and deal with the cause of these doubts and problems instead of getting caught up with the byproducts or symptoms. For example, many people struggle with procrastination, fear of failure, or self-sabotage, but these obstacles aren't the problem. The challenge is to discover *why* we are using procrastination in our life. How is it helping us cope with something else? We must drill down beyond what we see on the surface and look into the deep recesses of our hearts. Once there, we most often find fear and shame running rampant, cutting off circulation to our life source of imagination and activation.

I want a life that is less about maintenance and preoccupation with self and more about having a positive impact on others, changing the world around me, and allowing God's Spirit to do the moving. How do we get from a life of merely surviving to a life of thriving, while also in a place of peace and rest? In order for us to impact our community, the lives of others around us, and the world at large, we have to leave the mode of managing our own self-destruction. If we are busy 100 percent of the time on ourselves, we don't have any room for anyone else. Let's embrace leaving the camp of self, and let's hunt down the fears and shame that keep us from living the life we are destined to live!

THE GOAL AND PREFERRED OUTCOME

Our heart, which I also refer to as "the child within" or "the kid in you," is yearning to live with permission and without walls. This is what I call the sweet spot: living the true self without barriers or hindrances. If we don't live in our calling, we live someone else's life or a life that doesn't have purpose. Living a purposeless life creates a daily haunting of resentment and bitterness. We aren't living as our true selves. We either live in maintenance and management, or we can live on purpose and with impact.

I had to get the focus of my life off of managing fear and shame so that I could focus on fruitful living. This means doing what I love without looking over my shoulder; loving my wife and kids without second-guessing myself; not having to deal with the feeling of massive shame for not living up to my standards as a husband and parent; and being able to love God without trying to earn His love through my acceptable performances.

My struggle with fear and shame became overwhelming the moment my success started becoming public. When my career and my events started being recognized on an international scale, I got a stage fright type of feeling. I got to the root cause of this feeling and removed it. Life has never been the same, and my mental capacity has been freed up to enjoy what I was created to do.

How long have these problems been in your life? When did fear take hold in your life? What would your life look like without fear, anxiety, and worry? Would it get you closer to a full life? Pause a second and take a quick measurement.

#HUNTING TARGETS

There will be brief questions at the end of each chapter to poke and prod your mind and heart to get a tangible response from you. Use these questions as a tool to get some of your thoughts on paper. Otherwise, doubts will remain in your head and continue to stifle you. I started journaling in the mid-1990s, and it's been vital to my effectiveness and strategic living. I encourage you to keep a journal with the answers to these questions. This record will allow you to measure your growth as you learn to hunt fear and shame.

1. What motivated you to purchase this book? What areas of your life are driving you crazy? What part of "you" do you not like?

2. What do you fear most?

3. What does the ideal you look like?

4. What are the thoughts, beliefs, and mindsets that you constantly agree with that daily keep you from your ideal self and truthful living?

#CHAPTER 3

DEFINING THE ENEMY: WHAT IS FEAR? WHAT IS SHAME?

Our deepest fear is not that we are inadequate. Our deepest fear is that we are powerful beyond measure. It is our light, not our darkness, that most frightens us.' We ask ourselves, Who am I to be brilliant, gorgeous, talented, fabulous? Actually, who are you not to be? You are a child of God. Your playing small doesn't serve the world. There's nothing enlightened about shrinking so that other people won't feel insecure around you. We are all meant to shine, as children do. We were born to make manifest the glory of God that is within us. It's not just in some of us; it's in everyone. And as we let our own light shine, we subconsciously give other people permission to do the same. As we're liberated from our own fear, our presence automatically liberates others.[3]

MARIANNE WILLIAMSON

Being successful isn't necessarily about always making good decisions; often it's about making choices without being afraid to fail or afraid to make bad choices.

NOAH

ONE OF MY FAVORITE PASSIONS IN LIFE IS CREATING a brand architecture for people and their businesses. This isn't limited to their career, as I believe that we are each individually our own unique brand. It is our job to discover who we are, what we are supposed to do with our time here, and how we are supposed to do it with total peace of mind. Once we make these discoveries, we assemble them as a cohesive identity of our true self. This is our "brand."

As I've met with individuals, the common denominator of those who lead amazing, high-impact lives and those who don't is the crippling presence of fear and shame. The ones who go big are the ones who are fearless. The key for these successful people is that fear doesn't keep them from going after what they want to accomplish. Being successful isn't necessarily about always making good decisions; often it's about making choices without being afraid to fail or to make bad choices. What we believe changes the course of our behaviors and actions. If we tell ourselves we are worthless, or that we are limited because we come from a bad family or social status, then this will be our reality. However, if we tell ourselves that we are children of God, that we have a lot to offer, and that we are growing and becoming amazing people, our lives will begin to reflect these beliefs. It's amazing how powerful our minds and beliefs are in determining our destiny.

Are your decisions based on fears and lies? If they are, then fear is definitely your enemy. It's crucial to know what and who we are fighting—you cannot wage war if you don't have a strategy and don't know your enemy's tactics. Let's define our enemy so that we can effectively attack it.

For our purposes, we will give fear four different meanings—(1) traditional fear, (2) fear as a result of false evidence, (3) healthy fear, and (4) unhealthy fear.

Fear is traditionally defined in the following way:

fear [fi(ə)r]

noun

an unpleasant emotion caused by the belief that someone or something is dangerous, likely to cause pain or a threat: archaic—a mixed feeling of dread and reverence: *the love and fear of God.*

• (fear for) a feeling of anxiety concerning the outcome of something or the safety and well-being of • the likelihood of something unwelcome happening: she could observe the other guests without too much fear of attracting attention.

But I prefer to add my own spin to defining fear. I use the acronym:

False

Evidence

Appearing

Real

We often buy into façades that appear real when in fact they are a figment of our imaginations that lead us into actually believing the lies that we tell ourselves.

The key word in the dictionary definition is that fear is a belief, and usually it's a false belief. The amazing thing is that what appears as a massive demon or monster is often a paper tiger—nothing at all. We believe in something that is so thin that you can blow it over with your breath. The crazy thing is that it's all in our imagination. Whether it's the confronting phone call with a boss or friend, a negotiation in a business meeting, the test at school, the talk with parents, the work of art, the manuscript, the performance on stage, etc., all the fears that surround these moments are usually paper thin. They never are as big as they truly seem, and the situations never happen or get resolved in the way we imagine. Our mind can continually make problems in our head bigger than they truly are (False Evidence Appearing Real).

Some fears are healthy. For example, you want your children to have a healthy fear of real danger so that they will make wise choices to avoid injury. Another example of healthy fear is that of fearing God out of reverence and awe or having a healthy fear of authority. This type of fear is also the way children fear their parents in a positive way that brings correction, direction, and discipline where necessary.

In this book, we are tackling unhealthy fears that create faulty thoughts and beliefs—false evidence made to appear and then conceived as real. These fears influence us into changing our behaviors, which in turn change our decisions and actions. Thus, these fears manifest a life built on lies.

Scripture tells us, "There is no fear in love. But perfect love drives out fear because fear has to do with punishment. The one who fears is not made perfect in love" (1 John 4:18, NIV). If fear has to do with punishment, then by choosing fear, we are choosing to punish ourselves. It's time to ask, "Why? Why do we punish ourselves? Why do we *choose* to punish ourselves?" which turn into actions that we take on a regular basis that define our very lives. Once we make the connection that our beliefs determine our lives, we need to make sure that our beliefs are accurate and intentional.

I introduced my friend Jim in the first chapter because I believe that Jim's story is profound. He made decisions to confront his current boss and company, laying out what he wanted. He knew what he wanted and needed in life going into the meeting, and that made the confrontation easier because he was in the driver's seat. Even if he lost his job, a better one was waiting for him—the one he was creating for himself.

Although he spent a majority of his days before the meeting imagining how it was going to go, Jim said the meeting went completely differently than what he imagined (it always does). We imagine how the room will look, where people will sit, what people will say, etc., but it never plays out the way we imagine. Jim bravely presented his wishes and terms and they *declined* him! This forced Jim into a life of the unknown. This is what people fear the most—the unknown. Jim had a wife at home and two kids he needed to provide for. Jim interpreted this as freedom instead of fear. He saw this new opportunity to strike out on his own as being better than being trapped by a job with no future, making someone else money and keeping his dreams at bay.

Jim decided to face all of his fears and to create the new career that he wanted. This meant calling people in his industry and pulling together the connections and resources he needed. These calls took guts and courage; however, during the whiteboard session, he and I mapped out the reward that stood on the other side of his fears. I was able to walk Jim through this process because I used to be a person who wouldn't face fear, shame, and confrontation. I never knew the reward of freedom that was available to me as a result. Remember, if our dreams aren't intimidating to us, they are most likely too small and will not require much faith.

As we continued to work toward authenticity, Jim's heart became restless. He wanted more than revenue. He wanted meaning and value. He wanted purpose. Jim wanted to do what he was doing for his own company, not someone else's. As we hunt and master the art of fear hunting, it gives us the self-worth and permission to ask for what our hearts want and need. Today, Jim is forming his own company and stewarding his calling according to his desires, passions, core values, and family dreams. This is the sweet spot. Now, imagine if he had not made the decision to take action on hunting his fears. He would be settling to live in the status quo and would be run by fear and shame. His life would be based on a false pretense. He would be living someone else's life.

It's important to not continue to try and fix the areas in which we are broken; we face diminishing returns when we try to gradually get better in areas that we do not naturally gravitate toward. Rather, we should be focusing our energies toward our strengths and in the areas where we excel. Being a fearhunter frees you up to pursue the truth of who you are and to turn away from living someone else's life and reach for an authentic life that reflects your values and purpose.

In Steven Pressfield's book, *The War of Art*, he describes what he calls "resistance." Whether you call it resistance, fear, or the false self, this resistance is the enemy. Pressfield's book was a profound picture of the process I had lived for many years; I simply didn't have the words to describe it. I usually just blamed the world and others for my situation. I was a living victim of my past and circumstances. I felt like a pinball in a machine getting thrown around, living my life on the defense rather than on the offense.

Pressfield suggests that we can fight this resistance and move from the defense to the offense by what he calls *doing*. Pressfield's case for *doing* is a strong one. Fear's enemy is action. He claims that the louder and harder resistance shows up, it signifies that you are moving closer to your calling and true self. So the stress and fear, or resistance, is a signal that can also be used as a positive. It is critical to understand why the resistance only shows up at certain times. It typically doesn't show up when people are doing simple tasks. It often shows up when executing on a new idea requires that your heart is on display. Having your heart on display requires facing the unknown and overcoming personal doubts, insecurities, and the possibility of failure. Recognizing the arrival of resistance is critical to understanding how to defeat it—it's mere presence could mean that you are doing exactly what you are supposed to be doing!

Out of the necessity to survive mentally and emotionally, I had unknowingly adopted Pressfield's techniques of *doing* when I was young. When *The War of Art* showed up in my life, it finally put a name to what I was dealing with. I knew I could overcome resistance by *doing*, but I still needed to get down to the root of my defense mechanisms.

As a kid, I played a lot of video games. My youth was the dawn of the digital age, and it was the grand opening time for arcades. I remember games that had dinosaurs and a war game where you were a single shooter blasting anything that came at you. It was exhausting because the game never really ran out of enemy targets to shoot. They just kept coming like ants at a picnic. As my life shifted to overcoming and the art of *doing* every day, it became exhausting. Life felt like a nonstop barrage attacking my head.

When I was 14, I had to start working on the weekends to earn money. It might as well have been boot camp. This wasn't a paper route or something fun. I worked in my grandfather's machine shop washing out old oil pumps that you would find in gas stations and oil changing shops. To this day, it was the hardest and most brutal work I have ever done. While out in 100-plus degree heat, I would clean, wash, and repaint these tanks to be resold by my grandfather. I cried almost every day. I worked by myself and learned how to overcome because I needed the money—there were no handouts. I would come home with cuts all over my hands that stung from the solvent I used to clean the tanks. Overcoming this negative situation became my new discipline; however, knowing that I could overcome wasn't the answer to removing the fear and shame from my head. My issues couldn't be solved with a mind-over-matter attitude. Life became like the video game: I would show up each day in my head and just keep firing at the enemy of fears, lies, shame, and self-doubt. I spent my whole day managing self-talk rather than living my dream of being my true authentic self. I had no time to do anything fun and couldn't rest because I was too busy firing at the onslaught of the enemy.

Taking action, or *doing,* has its place in being self-disciplined, and for some, just this act alone will help them overcome the resistance or interference in their heads. In my case, fear was quieted, but the process of *doing,* or overcoming, was exhausting. If you do this long enough, you will burn out, which opens the door for depression and self-hate to take on incredible forms, taking root in your beliefs, actions, and habits. I realized that silencing fear in this way wasn't sustainable. I became passionate about finding true freedom—freedom from the constant roller coaster of thoughts that invaded my mind and the ways they held me back from my true self and identity. The way to get free is to take out the guys in the tower and the commanding officer—not the troops. I had to get to the root of why there was an enemy in the first place and why I had accepted playing this virtual video game in my head as an option.

There will be an invitation for you to discover these passions and your calling toward the end of the book. But for now, recognize that many of us have wasted a majority of our lives not building our dreams due to the fact we don't know how to get a true, passionate life. How do we find one?

#HUNTING TARGETS

1. What do you fear most in your current season?

2. When you think of the fears you have written down, what allows these fears to exist? What do you fear you will lose and what is the worst-case scenario if they come true?

3. On a scale of 1-10, how likely is it that any of these fears can or would come to fruition?

4. Take on the perspective of the child within you and look at these fears. If you got quiet for a moment and talked to him or her inside of you, what would he or she say about the fears or threats? Make sure to write down the feelings and responses.

#CHAPTER 4

THE ENEMY'S CO-CONSPIRATOR: THE FALSE SELF

Don't let your wounds make you become someone you're not.[4]

DEMI MOORE, ACTRESS

The false self within us tries to protect us from failure.

NOAH

FEAR DOES NOT STAND AS THE LONE ENEMY; WE HAVE been taken captive and are now co-conspirators with fear. My false self wages war to keep me from who I really want to be. The enemy of the true me is the enemy within born from past issues—the past issues that we accept and make agreements with. Our false self grows with each little lie that we believe. Why does the enemy within wage war against me? The false me is a protection mechanism aimed at keeping me safe from harm. The true me, the child within, doesn't want to feel bad or feel punished or lose connection, so I seek the familiarity of the past that comes from the false self rather than risk the uncertainty that comes from the unknown future that my true nature craves.

For example, the true self advises me to go sit with a cup of tea after I put the kids down and journal ideas for my next book or my new series of paintings. It encourages me to live productively, authentically, and with purpose. Then the false self says, "Why not just grab two pints of ice cream and camp out in front of the TV to watch Jimmy Fallon?" The reason why my head would usually pick the ice cream and TV is because it's a way to mask the risk of shame I might feel when I fail at writing, painting, and venturing into the unknown.

It's the same when I paint in the studio. My creativity and other ventures are risky and require work. If I choose to watch TV and eat ice cream, I'll feel ashamed that I made that choice and that shame acts as a false security: going to bed in a carb coma, waking up to feel like junk from a sugar hangover, thus causing me to have to work out to atone for making decisions that I later regretted. The mental roller coaster of this cycle creates a false identity to distract my attention from the vulnerability of nurturing my true self. Although the ice cream and Fallon will give me a quick connection and nurturance, it isn't sustaining and life-giving. That form of comfort in excess is damaging. That's why my soul wrestles. More importantly, it might be entertaining, but I lose the opportunity to build something fruitful and productive.

We have limited time on earth, and I've realized that I don't have much time to waste. Every minute of each day matters. There are certain recreational things that I do, but my soul has become disenchanted with the allure of chilling out in front of the TV when there are so many great things I can be working on in my life. I believe many people don't come home after five o'clock and begin working on passion projects because they don't know what their passions are. We have an internal resistance in this area because our false self is not allowing us to connect with our true passions.

I remember the week Chantel and I were heading back from a trip in the San Francisco Bay area after visiting some friends. As I drove, I listened to music and tried to vision cast my dreams. I kept coming back to the true, authentic questions, "Am I living my true, authentic self? In what areas of my life am I not being authentic and true and why not?" This assessment was very revealing. Around every corner of every thought was fear. As I faced and questioned every fear, I saw myself beheading the fear only to find the queen of fear standing there: shame. Every worst-case scenario I imagined in my head went back to what I believed about myself. I was sick to my stomach for the way I saw myself. I had to get down to business discovering, exposing, and eliminating the shame.

Let me give you an example of how the false self showed up during this drive. I asked myself, "What would happen if

I created part-time for clients and partners and shifted into doing what I love 80 percent of the time?" Immediately fear said, "Your income will go down. People won't buy it. It's already been done. You're too late in life. You will be rejected and nobody will follow you on social media anymore. You'll be a has-been. You won't get to stay in this house as a result. Your wife will be mad at you and you'll hate yourself for wasting time." Wow. That's a lot of negative self-talk! Where did that voice come from?! That voice is the false self within us trying to protect us from failure. This safety mechanism can help us think through possible outcomes; however, this voice is usually not a healthy friend. We have to stop and ask why we talk to ourselves this way before we get emotionally intoxicated, or drunk on fear.

The false self works hand in hand with fear to stop us from living authentically. Our goal is to encourage the true self to manifest in all that we do and to destroy the fear that feeds our false self.

#HUNTING TARGETS

1. Think of your biggest dreams as if you won the lottery. Write out your dream life and how you would spend an ideal week. This is the kind of week after you've done all the amazing travel and fantastic events. I'm talking about the ideal week: doing work and activities you love, spending time with family, and building relationships.

2. What happened to your heart while you wrote this ideal week out?

FLIP OVER YOUR PAPER.

3. What self-talk came up as you wrote out these dreams and ideas? What negative things did you hear?

4. What patterns and themes do you see in the self-talk?

5. What was happening in your life the first time you remember hearing this self-talk?

6. This might take some concentration, digging way back into your childhood. The past contains the keys to unlocking your shame and fear. Unlocking these locks will set you free from the mental prison you are in. Talk to yourself and your heart. This journey is the key. Right now work to discover. Write it out and repeat the first four hunting targets. You'll start to peel back the layers and find hidden gold within yourself.

#CHAPTER 5

HOW DOES THE ENEMY FIGHT?

A fear of the unknown keeps a lot of people from leaving bad situations.[5]

KATHIE LEE GIFFORD, TALK SHOW HOST

The false self is rooted in the fear of the unknown, not based on an objective reality.

NOAH

IN THE LAST CHAPTER, WE WORKED THROUGH THE importance of recognizing the false self's role in attempting to protect us but often hindering the development of our true self. It's crucial to remember that the false self is rooted in the fear of the unknown, not based on an objective reality. When the true, authentic self is free to be who he or she is called to be, that light of truth doesn't allow for the darkness of lies to exist.

The false self serves as a protection mechanism. Hunting the false self requires going to the root causes in the past where lies were born and vows were made as a child. Let me give you a general example of these powerful vows. A girl grows up with a demanding and oppressive mother and makes the vow that she will never become like her mother. An unhealthy focus on avoiding these negative traits can become her life's mission and therefore her false identity. The focus on avoiding the negative hinders the positive development of her true identity.

Often, there would be moments right before I wanted to do something that my heart was excited about when the enemy would start throwing everything it had at me. Once there was an event that I wanted to hold for the collectors of my artwork. The idea was to invite everyone to this location, put them all up in a hotel, and then provide fine dining while revealing all my newest pieces of art, and I planned to tell them the stories behind every piece. The moment I had this vision, I got sick to my stomach. I took inventory on my thoughts and came to the conclusion that if I was this nervous about the event, then it must be the right thing to do, and I became determined to do it. I became fearless. I gave myself permission to call the shots in creating the event of my dreams. I picked the best rooms, the best place to eat, and even bought gift bags for all the attendees. As the time approached, the doubts crept in. "Would they come? Would they like the work?" I pondered the outcome as I realized all the risk involved in hosting this event—both financially and in the vulnerability of this uncharted territory.

To live as your true self, give yourself permission to live from your heart and be prepared to dismantle the lies that crop up as a result of your brave thinking. These were the lies I slew in the above example: "They won't come. They will cancel. They won't buy. They will think you are crazy." My true self said, "Build it. Invite them. Be real. Design it the way you want." And more importantly, "Find out why you tell yourself these lies!"

The result? I only received one cancellation. Many of the event attendees were crying as they heard the meaning behind the pieces. I remember looking at my wife and saying, "This is our life. This is what we are supposed to be doing." We immediately started planning our second event. Imagine if I had listened to the lies instead of trying to fight against the enemy?

In order to be equipped to fight against these lies, we must be able to recognize them. What follows below and in the next chapter is an exploration of some of the fear-filled lies that the enemy uses to attack us. Remember, the better we can identify the enemy's tactics, the more effective we will be at fending off the attack.

FEAR OF FAILURE: THE GRANDDADDY OF THEM ALL

Failure exposes the path to success.

The amount of fear is proportional to the size of the risk.

Failure is an indicator of action.

Failure is one of the top fears that prevent people from moving into the life they want to live. Failure accomplishes this through the lies it produces. Whether it's the musician about to write a new song or album or someone wanting to quit their secure job to go out on a new venture, the idea of starting something unknown and unfamiliar is paralyzing. Thoughts of what *might* happen cripple the person to the point that they don't make a move. I have experienced this paralysis many times.

In the beginning of my career, I was gripped with fear whenever I embarked on creating a new series of art. It meant trying and experimenting, and I could fail drastically, wasting time on something that didn't work. Thirty years later I can tell you that there is actually no such thing as failure. Failure teaches us: it reveals what doesn't work. It is that simple. Failure exposes the path to success. The harder I painted and tried, the quicker I failed. And the quicker I failed, the sooner I discovered what was successful.

As a mentor, I have built the embracing of failure into my curriculum. I spend a majority of my mentoring time with companies and individuals helping them become professional failures. Successful people have this mindset wired into their DNA. They realize life is short, time is hunting them down, and the sooner they fail, the faster they will find and continue on their path of success.

The story of Donna is a perfect example. Donna was an artist living with her husband and two children. For years, she had spent her days creating artwork that sold well. She created abstract paintings on canvas that were popular with designers and in fashion. Her challenge was that she made her living creating and selling each original work. This business model is difficult to scale and can limit freedom in the work schedule. During a strategy session, I explained the concept of publishing work through limited edition prints and posters. Applying this strategy to her business scared her. She didn't think her collectors would buy prints, and she didn't want to interrupt the flow of life with a new system. What if it failed?

I wanted her to focus on her goal: make enough passive income so that she had the freedom to live life and make memories with her family. Accomplishing these goals would require moving away from the old model of painting an original work in order to make a dollar. The key was to have her develop products to add to her website. After explaining the many benefits, she began to understand the power of this concept. The prize and reward were worth walking through the fear of failing.

The real concerns she had to face were the practical ones, such as manufacturing, pricing, vendors, shipping, customer service, and packaging. We gathered that information and she began to execute each step. This process took several days, but once she had the resources, it was just a matter of making phone calls and getting things done.

We can dream and cast visions, but the key is to make our dreams a reality through building and executing. Otherwise, our dreams are only empty goals with no deadlines and nothing becomes a reality. Fear wins when we believe the lie. The lie tells us we will fail if we step into our dreams. Eventually, regret sets in and we heap up piles of self-hate while wondering what could have been.

Donna was generating revenue from her online store within the first three months of changing her business model. She began to dismantle any fear that crept into her mind because she knew that reward awaited her on the other side of fear. Her collectors were happy, she was happy, and her husband was happy. Most importantly, she could take a break from the easel and be with her loved ones. Notice how easily the paper tigers of fear were blown away by a breakthrough in her thinking. None of this would have happened unless she had created the ideal situation for her craft. This creation took decisions of faith and courage. With each action and step, she became a fearhunter. I am excited to see what takes place in her future as she hunts bigger game: bigger dreams, bigger risks, bigger failures, and bigger successes.

If you are about to embark on a new journey serving at your church or helping someone launch a business selling things on eBay, you might not have much resistance or fear because there is minimal risk involved. But if you are going to write a book on facing fear, stand on stage and give a public speech, or release your new song, then that's a whole other story. Why? Because those tasks require being vulnerable and facing the risk of failure. The amount of fear is proportional to the size of the risk.

The fear of exposure—being seen—is a major component in facing the fear of failure. This is also where shame piggybacks on fear and says, "You are who you are based on what you do." If you fail, you're a failure; if you succeed, you're a success. Shame wants you to believe that your worth and identity are based on your performance. That was me. Shame me and I'll jump through hoops to please you, win your favor, acceptance, love, and connection. It took serious identity work to discover the identity on which my whole life was hanging, and one day it finally clicked as I was working with one of my mentors. Despite shame's performance-based system of determining value, I was set free by the truth that my identity in God is based on my intrinsic value and worth as a human and not based on what I do. This truth has changed my life, and I hope that it also provides you as much freedom as it has me. I don't have to spend my days striving, looking to earn connection, love, and compassion. I have it in my heavenly Father. His grace is sufficient. I can't earn or perform to get it.

Failure is a beast of a fear because of the implication of permanence involved; we don't want failure to go on our record. When I was 23 years old, I painted a new series that I was really excited about and was very curious about how each piece would be received. I didn't know if it was good work in view of the critics and the industry standard. I wanted to get an honest opinion from someone who could give me critical feedback.

I took several of these paintings and drove to a gallery nearby where I wanted to be featured. I walked in and met the woman who owned the gallery and asked if I could show her my work, and she agreed. As I displayed each piece, her assistant sat there with her. He was a tall, lanky man. They were both posh and intimidating. I think she was a little taken aback that a young, 20-something was bringing in work for an opinion. What she said next was crucial to my career as a creative: "Your work technique is one of the highest I have ever witnessed for portraits and the human body; however, I want a painting that I can look at longer than enjoying a cigarette." That statement cut me to the core. She praised my technique and style but identified that there wasn't enough substance and storytelling. I had created fast food. This standard became a mantra and measuring stick for myself as I grew my career and craft. If I was going to create anything worthwhile, it would need to have my heart in it. It would need to have substance and a lasting nurturance.

So was the gallery visit a failure? Was she correct in rejecting my work? Was her opinion worth listening to? While some would see this gallery visit as a failure, I looked at it as an opportunity to be refined. One of my passions is learning, so this encounter actually fueled me. That day at the gallery was fifteen minutes, but it changed the rest of my life. My work needed storytelling and authenticity, and I was determined to deliver. I needed to create work that connected on a heart level and wasn't just cool. It later gave me the idea for the term "fast food art": It tastes great, but it doesn't have any long-lasting nourishment.

My life changed when I made failure my friend. In fact, if I wasn't failing, I wasn't moving forward or growing. Failure is an indicator of action, but I also have to be careful that I'm not taking action by only doing work that is safe. The goal is to grow and stretch. It is similar to exercise: yesterday I ran three miles, and today I ran 3.2 miles. I had to embrace the fact that truly living requires being in a constant state of discomfort. A true, meaningful, and faithful life demands dreaming, building, and doing, but failure is also, ironically, a crucial element to embrace. My personal goal has been to outdo myself, yet I'm not here to please myself; my greatest customer is God—the one who gave me the gift of creativity in the first place.

Failure is the best teacher. My craft has been refined, my marriage is better, and the course of my parenting corrected because I'm always looking to improve on them. If you'd like to lead a life of impact and growth, I would suggest embracing failure as one of your greatest allies. It's a sign that you truly are growing. Failure allows you to become fearless and stare at the biggest giants with total confidence. This is how ridiculous dreams are born and conquered. Many people won't even allow themselves the permission to dream due to their fear of failure. I want to encourage you to stop dictating your future in light of your past. Your past and the fears that have been born from it have kept you from the life you want to live in the present and the future. You have a choice: either fear can be in control of your true self and authentic living, or you can take the reins and live your dreams.

Even as I have recognized fear and chosen to fight back and press into my dreams, have the lies stopped? No. Why? Because I keep growing as a fearhunter, going bigger on the assignments God keeps presenting. The closer you come to your true self, the bigger the lies that show up to knock you down. However, I promise you that the more you continue to walk in your true self, the less you listen to the false self.

Grab your pen and journal and answer a few of these questions as an exercise to dig down into some of the lies and fears that are holding you back.

#HUNTING TARGETS

1. What are some of the messages that you listen to every day regarding your success?

2. Define success. Write it down. Where did you get this definition? The world? Your school? The culture?

3. Is your life's meaning, value, and worth contingent on a vacation, car, and house?

4. What hobby/activity/work do you love so much that you would do it for free?

5. What are some of the recurring self-doubts that pop into your head when you are working on something that you are passionate about?

6. Do you ever let these fears/lies stop you from doing what you desire to do? Give an example.

7. When you think of the word "failure" as it relates to you, what areas come to mind? Why?

8. Where is the message of the failure coming from? Others? What were you told as a kid about failure? Do other people's words trigger past issues and memories?

9. What failures in your life have you learned from?

10. Does the idea of failure make you lock up with fear? Do you feel it has kept you from truly living?

11. What does a life that embraces failure look like for you? Does it include confrontation? Risk? Being truthful? Living authentically? Not worrying about what others think?

#CHAPTER 6

COUNTERATTACK: FEAR-BASED SYMPTOMS DEBUNKED

Apple Computer would not have reached its current peak of success if it had feared to roll the dice and launch products that didn't always hit the mark. In the mid-1990s, the company was considered washed up. Steve Jobs had departed, and a string of lackluster product launches unrelated to the company's core business had failed to catch fire.[6]

NAVEEN JAIN, EXECUTIVE, ENTREPRENEUR

The shackles have been undone and the jail cell has swung wide open, yet man chooses to remain in the familiar, paralyzed by fear of the unknown.

NOAH

IN THE PREVIOUS CHAPTER, WE DISCUSSED THE FEAR OF failure—the granddaddy of all fears. There are many other common fears, and their byproducts, that plague us every day. Often we unconsciously make thousands of agreements with lies based on fears. So let's explore some other common fears and the lies that accompany them. Below are some of the conventional fears we encounter:

Fear of Success

Procrastination

Self-Sabotage

What Others Think of Us

Fear of Confrontation

Fear that You're Not Good Enough (Victimization)

Fear of Change

Fear of Embarrassment

The fear of the unknown is the foundation of most of the fears discussed below. We often fear what we can't see. This is based on wanting to be in control, and ultimately, to feel safe. The shackles have been undone and the jail cell has swung wide open, yet man chooses to remain in the familiar, paralyzed by fear of the unknown. Keep this underlying fear in mind as we explore the other fears below.

FEAR OF SUCCESS

The fear of success is rooted in the fear of responsibility and the action required to manage it. I believe that a majority of folks fear success because they haven't defined success, and they don't know what they would do with it if they had it. My fear was about the unknown of success—how to handle a team, payroll, money, etc. You may have never been in a position of success before, so it's naturally going to be daunting and scary. I think it's amazing that people would rather stay in the prison of inaction than face uncomfortable questions such as, "What would I do with an increase in money and the lives that I will impact if I became successful?" Yet I also feared the responsibility of success. This was the fear of the unknown. I began to get angry and frustrated that I was allowing this fear to hold me back. Maybe I didn't have the know-how or the wisdom I needed, but I knew I wanted it. I didn't want the fear of the unknown and fear of success to cripple me from the true life I had always dreamed of having.

I remember watching my mentors when I was a teenager. They were businessmen who lived dynamic lives. They had nice homes, nice cars, great marriages, and a balanced life. Faith in God was their guide, and they lived with purpose and intention. These guys didn't leave any meat on the bone of life. These men helped shape my definition of success. It wasn't the Donald Trump kind of success of suits and Wall Street. The guys I followed didn't measure their self-worth by their net worth. They were producers of significance. As I watched these men through the course of the next thirty years, I gained insight into significance, and I started asking what true success was and what it would take to achieve it.

As I modeled my life after these men, I defined success in my career as doing work of preferred content, with and around people I loved. Additionally, I used the abundance of revenue I earned to give to kingdom initiatives. I wanted my success to be defined through an eternal lens, not a temporal one. This idea of success changed everything in terms of facing fears and the risk of success because the questions that surrounded the unknown had been answered. I was energized by the idea that "success" was defined by doing my best work while surrounded by amazing people and helping others, all while growing the kingdom.

Fear of the unknown, fear of responsibility, and even not knowing what your purpose and calling are can cause inaction that can turn into indifference and anxiety. This can be toxic, depressing, and ultimately unfruitful. The solution is to take action. Stepping into the unknown brings you closer to your true self because of the growth that occurs through stepping out in faith. You will find through action and growth that your life is actually the strategic solution for a lot of problems and needs around you. The longer you remain in fear, the longer you aren't producing the positive impact you were put there for.

PROCRASTINATION: ANALYSIS PARALYSIS

Procrastination is the fear of success. People procrastinate because they are afraid of the success that they know will result if they move ahead now. Because success is heavy, carries a responsibility with it, it is much easier to procrastinate and live on the "someday I'll" philosophy.[7]
DENIS WAITLEY, MOTIVATIONAL SPEAKER, AUTHOR

I have been in the business of creativity for the last thirty years of my career. As an artist, I spend the majority of my days dreaming up an idea and then bringing it to life in my studio. This is the hardest work I've ever done—not because the painting is tough but because of the time between dreaming and the art of doing. The dreaming and ideas are easy.

When I wrote my first book, I ran into many speed bumps created by my false self. There was a mountain of fear in my head: Who would want to read this? There are already so many books in the world. No one cares about my life story; people will think I'm egotistical. It was easy to dream about what I wanted to write, but it took everything in me to start because of these speed bumps; however, as soon as I started, it was off to the races. You couldn't stop me.

Procrastination is one of the biggest byproducts of fear because, again, we fear the unknown. The fear of lacking a certain skill set causes us to get stuck doing nothing. The state of doing nothing is less shameful than the fear of failing at our attempts. Nike is correct with their "Just Do It" slogan—we must begin the journey. The fears of our past say, "If you start, you may fail, and then lose connection with what your heart needs. If it succeeds, you will have to be responsible." You can see how this cycle can be so destructive.

SELF-SABOTAGE

The underbelly of the human psyche, what is often referred to as our dark side, is the origin of every act of self-sabotage. Birthed out of shame, fear, and denial, it misdirects our good intentions and drives us to unthinkable acts of self-destruction and not-so-unbelievable acts of self-sabotage.[8]

DEBBIE FORD, AUTHOR, COACH

Self-sabotage is essentially a fear of the unknown, but it more closely resembles a fear of success. As I've counseled creatives over the years, they say they wouldn't know how to handle the responsibility of new ventures. It's interesting for me to watch. A person dreams a dream. They embark on the journey of building, and taking steps to create the dream. They start to execute and then right before they launch, they shelf the idea or project. I have seen it all too often with independent small-business owners. They have a great idea and set out to build it, but then pull the plug just as it is about to catch some wind in the sails. My friend Jeff is a perfect example. Jeff is a talented photographer who loves shooting landscapes, lifestyle photography of friends, and portraits of his clients. Even though he is amazing at his craft, things changed as I counseled him on the idea of developing his own series to do a show. I could tell that he was a bit overwhelmed with the idea. It was as if he feared the exposure of being on a wall and people not buying his stuff. He was haunted by the uncertainty of what *might* happen.

Actualizing is a process by which we think through what might happen. This process is very evident in my life. As I've mentioned, events don't typically turn out the way we imagine they will. However, this process kept me from actually doing the work and putting it out in the world as a test. The art or idea never saw the light of day. This was also Jeff's challenge. Jeff wouldn't allow himself the chance to display his work. The false Jeff inside would rise up and shut it down out of fear of the loss of connection. The common thread of each fear we face is that we fear the unknown and what we can't control. However, the flip side is that we then make agreements with shame for not doing it. It's a vicious cycle.

I've worked with Jeff to create small incremental steps toward his goal of having a show to present his work. We started with clear expectations. We formed a list of desired outcomes for the event, such as creating the work he has always dreamt of, along with fulfilling the dream of having a show and creating the opportunity to generate additional income. The last point of making money is a subtle but important point. Most people define their success based on the revenue of the show or event. Jeff is defining his success so that even if he sells nothing, it isn't a failure. He is simply recognizing that he is creating an opportunity to make extra money. If he has a show and no one attends, it isn't a failure. If no one shows up and nothing sells, the event is still a success because he created the work he's always wanted to create, and he organized his first show. This mindset allows for two successes independent of whether people show up or any of his photography is sold.

Self-sabotage also plays into self-hate and/or the value of self. We tell ourselves, "I don't deserve this attention," or "I will be picked on." It's amazing to see how we have miniature versions of ourselves inside our heads. This is why I believe it is very important to be in tune with the kid in you. This kid is aware and is very much alive. The fact is that we can let that kid grow and flourish or we can allow him to curl up in a corner, sucking his thumb in fear. That kid isn't going to come out and flourish unless he feels safe to do so. You are the key to healing and helping this kid to come out and blessing us with their amazing heart.

Self-sabotage is also a defense mechanism. Our false self will rise up and slam shut the lid of our hopes and dreams out of fear of the unknown. Once you are aware of this pattern, you will be able to start digging and uproot it. The key is to rebuild from the wreckage of the bomb that happened in the past.

An example I often discuss is working out and eating. One is fuel and essential to staying alive and the other is essential to keeping fit. However, I used both as a way to numb myself from my true me. Working out was the worst possible thing I had to do on any given day, but the byproduct was profound in the way I felt about myself. I would normally self-sabotage by eating at night because it gave me a reason to have to work out. I know, it's lame. But when I would sit down at night and read a book or write instead of eating, it would create more momentum and value that was productive in my life. Again, I could see the person I wanted to be across the room as the ideal avatar of me, but it was safer to self-loathe and live in regret than it was to strive to be my ideal self.

Even though we don't master the disciplines of fear hunting immediately, there is a profound phenomenon that takes place the moment we change a decision: things are disrupted and things change. The course is altered. The goal is to continue altering the course. They say it takes twenty-one days to form or break a new habit. For me, I found that my "why" became my reasons for changing my behaviors. I began changing my routines and habits because I wanted more. I wanted to write books, I wanted to make films, I wanted a better body. I wanted to live longer to be with family and produce value for God and people. I wanted to live a life of thriving, not one of simply managing chaos and surviving. Riding the merry-go-round of self-sabotage is a place to camp out and hide. Get off the ride and engage the unknown.

WHAT OTHERS THINK OF US: FEARS ONLINE AND IN SOCIAL MEDIA

We tell lies when we are afraid ... afraid of what we don't know, afraid of what others will think, afraid of what will be found out about us. But every time we tell a lie, the thing that we fear grows stronger.[9]

TAD WILLIAMS, AUTHOR, COMIC BOOK WRITER

As I built my company from the time I was a young kid, I took every penny and made every effort to build the best product I could in order to best care for my customers. Early in my career, I traveled to various events within the art world, which included conventions and trade shows. I also taught courses in the industry on airbrushing and other art techniques. From a young age, I viewed branding and self-promotion as a tool to gain influence and market share (at 15, I had a comic strip and apparel line called Kyber Kalahan). This was during the '90s before social media and the Internet presence we enjoy today. Even during the pre-Internet age, I was beginning to be published and my brand was getting recognition. Even then I encountered feedback that wasn't only critical but was also downright hurtful and accusatory—things that would make people want to throw in the towel.

Today, haters and online bullies have put some people on the defensive, and others are completely afraid of sharing their work or their lives online. People hide behind false identities and then hurl insults and hate online. I've seen this paralyze people, creating a life of fear and added stress that wasn't there before. It's incredible how living in the digital age has made it so easy to get things done online, connect to more people, and allow us to be more easily accessible. On the flip side, the fear of being exposed, facing confrontation, saying what you really feel, being vulnerable, and putting your heart on display for the world has exponentially increased. How many times have you stopped before publishing a post and asked, "I wonder what they will think? Will they like me? Will I be accepted? Will this get shared?"

A lot of people fear success and the life they truly want out of fear of what others will do or say. Let me just tell you that if you gain momentum in your career and life, you are guaranteed to face resistance and haters. Being a leader puts you out in front of the pack, and being in front means that you will take the brunt of the arrows that are fired. Leading and being a pacesetter have a price. The price is facing criticism and being lonely. I have received threats on my life, haters on social media, and ridiculous comments on my blog.

The moment you break free in your thinking and begin to embark on becoming the real you, executing on your dreams and business, you may get a tsunami wave of resistance from your most immediate loved ones and friends. Your family might say you're crazy or that you are all about you. You may appear to be egotistical. I remember when I started blogging and getting my true voice out to the public, I was bombarded by haters. I had never seen or dealt with such criticism before. I put out something that was genuine and authentic, and it was trampled on.

Posting online makes you feel vulnerable and can initiate the whole process of self-sabotage again. Haters online have a field day hiding behind a fake avatar and firing arrows at those who are living the life they wish they had the guts to live.

(For those wondering what to do, I suggest not responding.) Taking something seriously from a hater is toxic. You are listening to someone who doesn't know you at all and giving them power over you.

What others think of me is none of my business. We can't live our lives in fear of what other people might think of us. Allowing this creates false idols in our lives by making others' opinions the measuring stick for our self-worth. To free yourself from hate and the negative comments slung at you requires dying to these concerns. You have to be willing to fail as big as possible without caring what others think. It means looking like a complete idiot to yourself and others without letting it paralyze you.

FEAR OF CONFRONTATION

> *Fear runs our lives. It doesn't matter who you are. You have to understand your relationship with fear. Whether you're scared of getting into a relationship or taking the new job or a confrontation—you have to size fear up.*[10]
>
> CHRIS PINE, ACTOR (JAMES T. KIRK, *STAR TREK*)

Fear of confrontation is one of the largest fears I've faced being self-employed. Whether you have to make a phone call and negotiate the deal or admit you blew it on a calculation, it is an area that no one likes because confrontation makes us uncomfortable.

Have you ever found yourself analyzing to death what might happen about a confrontational circumstance or event? So often we go through our days or weeks visualizing and actualizing what might happen, and it paralyzes our actions. Actualizing, if not handled wisely, can impair the mind and soul. The key to using this tool wisely is to ask yourself how terrible the outcome might really be on each step of the way. Very rarely, and I mean very rarely, does a situation turn out terribly or end in catastrophe. In William Backus and Marie Chapian's book, *Telling Yourself the Truth*, they describe the amazing effects of actualizing. They suggest literally walking through the steps, acting them out as if you take action and are rejected. Will you lose the job, not get the bid, get denied, or any number of outcomes? The question to ask is, what is the worst that could happen? You might not get paid, might not make more money, might not move, might not ... whatever. This over-actualizing is almost always present when we are called to confront someone or something in our life that needs changing.

In 2008, the entire world began to endure one of the largest economic downturns since the Great Depression. During this time, my family was not only affected by the economy, but we were also wrestling with many adversities in our personal life. We had three properties and a growing business. Chantel was self-employed at her hair salon as part owner, and I was self-employed working on my art. We received a huge blow upon learning that our son has special needs and is on the autism spectrum. Going to that meeting and getting him assessed was one of the hardest confrontations we've had to face as parents. Shortly after, we were challenged with real-estate investments going sideways, losing a home, moving, then my stepmother battling cancer and passing away. The decisions and seasons of the recession prompted Chantel and me to look at life differently.

I remember the night we officially became fearhunters and eliminated the fear of confrontation from our lives. We were on a date night at one of our favorite restaurants, and I asked Chantel, "If you could have your life any way you wanted, what would it look like? How would you spend your time and days?" She responded that she would sell her side of the partnership of the salon she co-owned so that she could work fewer days to be at home with our kids—to help more and to be more present. She wanted to keep doing hair, but she wanted to do it on her terms. Fear warned us that we would have to confront the other partners, that her clientele would drop off, and that we would lose a majority of her income. I told her that night, "Let's do it tomorrow!" Chantel and I didn't want to spend another day living lives that didn't make us happy and fulfilled. We were, and still are, willing to downsize and reduce expenses for the chance to free up time and have more time with the kids, despite the confrontation that it sometimes requires.

This sort of thinking and action require staring confrontation in the face and beheading it. Life is too short to not live the life you've always wanted. Too often we stay inactive out of fear of what others will do, say, or think of us. We are terrified of confrontation. I encourage you to believe that the life on the other side of confrontation is beyond worth it.

Chantel confronted the partners; it was a little stressful, but change is always a little messy, and we kept our eye on the prize. She began working two and a half days a week and made exactly what we needed. My business picked up additional revenue and the kids have more of both of us. It has been one of the scariest decisions we've ever made but also one of the most rewarding. We've never looked back.

Confrontation can be scary. I get it. You might as well ask the kid in you to go into an abandoned house on a dark street at midnight. It's scary, but it doesn't have to be immobilizing. Even today I have to keep my ax ready to behead the fears that stand in my way. Confrontation is an everyday opportunity to face relationships with truth. Being your true self and understanding your heart are worth battling for and sticking up for. People continually get depressed and angry because they are unsettled by what others have done, have said, or are doing. It shuts them down like kryptonite. They wake up and swallow the toxic pill of being non-confrontational, which makes them resentful and paralyzed. Meanwhile, they are so wrapped up in running damage control and hating themselves that they aren't living the productive life they truly want to live. They become angry at themselves because they know other people are dictating how they feel about themselves and how they live. Trust me. I know. I've been there and it's toxic; it's poison for the soul.

Confrontation and the fear of rejection are two of the most dealt-with fears due to the fact that many of us are in the mode of "selling" every day. In order to get the things we need, we have to ask. Asking is confronting, and it happens numerous times daily for me. Becoming a fearhunter creates courage. You'll find yourself asking "what if" more often and going outside the box for the life you want. Confrontation will be the new norm, and you will become less intimidated by it.

Confrontation is not going away if you choose to live as your true authentic self. It is inevitable. As I've become a fearhunter, confrontation has become a consistent element in my life. In order for you to become productive, you will be required to limit the people and circumstances that drain time and energy from your life. This comes at a cost and stirs things up. Through discipline, my schedule has become stricter, causing me to govern my time, which meant I became a "no" man. In the past, I was always saying "yes" to any request for fear of confrontation, but I realized that if I didn't start saying no, I wouldn't have any healthy boundaries. The moment I set boundaries for my creativity and my craft, I experienced resistance. This guaranteed confrontation is another reason why many people fear success.

FEAR OF CHANGE

The only thing I fear more than change is no change. The business of being static makes me nuts.[11]

TWYLA THARP, DANCER, CHOREOGRAPHER

I mostly hear about the fear of change as it pertains to the person who is looking for a new career or contemplating moving. Sometimes it comes up in relationships too. Chantel and I encountered the fear of change when we became fearhunters and sought out authentic, impactful living. We didn't want the status quo. We wanted change. Leaders don't feel like they are living unless they are seeking or dealing with change. Managers, however, avoid it like the plague.

There are those who live a life based on controlling the present, trying to make it as secure as possible. This subtle but powerful mode of living and state of mind can end up ruling your life. It is a misbelief that if you can just get enough money in the bank, your career more predictable, and everyone safe, then your life will be peaceful. When we think this way, it forms a false identity, and the hamster wheel required to meet these achievements becomes an idol in our life. We become more concerned about managing what we have rather than creating something new. Tim Ferriss discusses this in his book *The 4-Hour Work Week*: "We need to stop wasting our energy on keeping the money we have. Our energy is better spent finding out ways to make additional revenue." That statement changed my life. My life's energy had been spent managing money and living a life of scarcity. It gave me permission to be more courageous in the "ask" and in overcoming the fear of rejection.

People often make excuses for the way they are because they fear change. Some resort to looking at their family of origin as the cause for their current state. "My parents were fat, therefore, I am fat. They never had money, so I don't have money," and so the story goes. Now, one would argue that you are a product of your upbringing, but I am convinced that we get to choose our lives. If you can't stand where you are in life, then go beg a person whom you feel has their life in order for their advice and counsel or find a mentor who can help steer you in the right direction. One degree of change in the course of the Titanic would have kept the ship from a collision with disaster. One change in your habits and paradigms can change the course of your life, history, and even the future for your children.

FEAR OF BEING EMBARRASSED

Remembering that I'll be dead soon is the most important tool I've ever encountered to help me make the big choices in life. Because almost everything—all external expectations, all pride, all fear of embarrassment or failure—these things just fall away in the face of death, leaving only what is truly important.[12]

STEVE JOBS, COFOUNDER AND CEO, APPLE INC.

I recently walked through Times Square in New York, and I realized that I felt and viewed the world differently due to technology. When I was a child, there were only a few ways I could be embarrassed—with friends at school or maybe activities after school. Today, our lives are shared with millions of people online. Fear of being embarrassed doesn't lie with what we might do but more with what *others* might do or say. Sharing online is one example of how this fear can be overwhelming, but the opportunities for being embarrassed have been taken to a whole new level.

Embarrassing moments can often turn into endearing stories once some time has passed; it did for me as I remember one of the biggest days in my career. I was meeting with a certain division of one of the Fortune 500 companies I work with to get a licensing deal. I will never forget this day—I was fired up after spending a great deal of time preparing for the meeting. I have always been a believer that if you want to sell an idea and want people to invest emotionally, you have to give them proof that you believe in it yourself by creating an example of it. That said, I created several pieces to share my vision and strategies. As I sat in the meeting, I remember being really humbled and taken aback. I had dreamed of working with this company and being in the same buildings where some of the greatest creativity has ever been launched. I remember the feeling of nervousness because I really valued and respected their opinion. During the meeting, I remember thinking about what could happen if this actually got approved to move forward. It was pushing the boundaries of new art techniques and style not normally done in this division, so a green light would also move the division in a new direction.

The meeting went well and I walked out relieved. The pitch was approved, and we moved forward with a deal; however, as I walked out of the meeting and got in my car, I looked down as I buckled my seatbelt. I was horrified to discover that my zipper was wide open. Yes. You could have driven a freight train through it. A feeling of electric shock went through my entire body, and I sat there sick to my stomach. I kept saying out loud, "Oh no! Oh gosh, no, not today!! Of all days, not today!" I called the assistant that I knew pretty well and confronted her by asking if she noticed anything in the meeting or if her boss had said anything. She said, "No," and thought it was pretty funny. It took the seriousness of this life milestone out of the situation, but it left such an embarrassing mark on me that I've remembered it enough to write about it in this book. This incident taught me a lot about how God has a sense of humor when it comes to being proud and cocky. It reminded me to take things less seriously and to worry less about being embarrassed. Everyone is insecure; everyone is posing to some degree.

The fear of being embarrassed is one that locks up people on stage, especially when speaking live. Whenever I have speaking engagements, I am reminded of the courage it takes. It's easy to sit and watch people from the audience of life and say that you can do it better. It all changes when you're standing in front of thousands of people. It takes serious courage. If you don't risk, you can't succeed, and you'll never know what is possible. Coming to the realization that speaking is a gift to help other people enabled me overcome my fear of embarrassment. Filming a video for YouTube, speaking at a conference, or putting myself out there in some other way is an opportunity to help someone. As a creative, I've had to accept responsibility for my actions and risks. However, the outcome far outweighs the pain or embarrassment.

VICTIMIZATION

Our past may explain why we're suffering, but we must not use it as an excuse to stay in bondage.[13]

JOYCE MEYER, AUTHOR, SPEAKER

We live in a society of victimization, where people are much more comfortable being victimized than actually standing up for themselves.[14]

MARILYN MANSON, SHOCK ROCKER

Playing the victim gets exhausting. Eventually, you begin to realize that you blame your current situation on everyone else.

NOAH

As you can see, almost all of these examples of different fears interlink back to the same source: the fear of the unknown. We selfishly want to stay in the familiar rather than confront and break through the unknown. A common byproduct of the fear of the unknown is the "victim role." We camp out on this identity and go no further. Playing the victim is the equivalent of being codependent.

When I was dating in my 20s, I continuously had the same issues with all of the girls I picked. I was fully committed when it came to relationships, but to an unhealthy extent. I would lose myself in whomever I was with. I defined my identity by how much I took care of them, how pretty they were, and how well the relationship was going. I became codependent in each relationship. You can think of a codependent in this way: if a codependent were about to die, someone else's life would pass before their eyes instead of their own. That was me.

The common denominator in all of my failed relationships was me. It was a hard thing to admit and learn, but it was a harsh, true reality. It became so bad that I ended up in counseling. I had become a professional victim. My life was determined and defined by others, including those from my past. My present and my future looked bleak because I defined myself by all that had happened to me.

It's easy to play the victim, but it gets exhausting. Eventually, you begin to realize that you blame your current situation on everyone else. Many people living as victims *believe* that their situation is all there is. Their whole life and identity are based on the belief that they are victims of their past, their upbringing, their parents' authority, their school, their church, the amount of money in the bank—you name it. Yes, we might have been a victim in a certain situation, but we have the choice to decide whether or not that trauma is going to rule us or define us now and into the future. You can't change the past, but you certainly can change the present and the future. Your choices are the only things you have control over.

As I was first embarking on my career, I was in survival mode. Food, water, shelter and security rested on my shoulders. Failure became my friend in a good way. The more I failed, the closer I got to success. The secret was that I had to get over myself. I had to get over looking like an idiot. I remember going door to door and cold-calling people who needed commissioned artwork. This was a twofold exercise in failure: I was worried they would say no, and I was also worried that if they said yes, they wouldn't like what I had created, leaving my heart vulnerable. I embraced this process because I was in survival mode and didn't have the luxury to let fear stop me. I became fearless. Yes, I experienced loss and failure, but fear was optional. How terrible could it be? They could say no and my feelings or ego would be a little bruised. Or they could say the painting wasn't good and I would be embarrassed. What is the worst outcome? Loss of income and maybe loss of dignity? The greater principle learned was risk versus reward; I would stretch myself into new territory on technique, people skills, adding to my portfolio, and it would even pay the bills. In learning these principles, I broke the cycle in our family history. There are creatives in our family, but most of them had flatlined due to self-sabotage, analysis paralysis, and fear. I was now creating my future rather than playing the victim.

Most individuals will look at the carnage of their life and think they have already missed their window of opportunity or feel that they're not good enough to take hold of the life they want. Fear jumps in the way. We fear the unknown of what's on the other side of being our true selves and taking ownership in our lives for what we want. When I came to this crossroads, I reflected on my talks with Chantel, complaining about how I was sick and tired of being sick and tired. It seemed like everyone else had no problem being and saying what they wanted, so why was I tiptoeing around life in fear of how people might respond or what people might say? It was time to start swinging the sword of truth to behead the lies and misbeliefs that I had agreed with.

#HUNTING TARGETS

1. Do you fear success? Why?

2. Imagine yourself standing in your kitchen as you live a successful life. What does that person look like? What does this person manage? What are they in charge of?

3. What mental pictures come to mind when you see this ideal, successful you?

4. Are the fears of success that you imagined really terrible or just undefined? Write it out in your journal.

5. The ultimate test to find out if you are living your true self and being the *real you* on a daily basis is to ask those who know you best: your family, coworkers, friends, your tribe online. Journal your first reaction.

6. Do you fear change?

7. In what ways do you feel you are playing the victim? Are there areas in your life you hold on to as the victim? Write them out.

8. What areas do you see yourself using self-sabotage? Do you notice a cycle?

9. When it comes to confrontation, what is your normal approach? Do you retreat?

#CHAPTER 7

ENEMY BATTLEGROUND: THE POWER OF CHOICE

And do not be conformed to this world, but be transformed by the renewing of your mind, so that you may prove what the will of God is, that which is good and acceptable and perfect.

PAUL THE APOSTLE (ROMANS 12:2)

The best way to predict the future is to invent it.[15]

ALAN KAY, COMPUTER SCIENTIST

You cannot expect positive results in life when you believe negative things about yourself.

NOAH

I WAS IN THE STUDIO IN PRODUCTION ON A CHALLENGING day. I took a break and went into the kitchen for a cup of tea. As I sat there, I had the realization that the difference between other people and myself is the decisions we make. I know it seems trivial, but that idea clicked. It was like I was electrocuted in truth. I can choose how I want my life to go. Nobody is holding me back but me. I then thought about my life and about the results that others were getting. I wanted more. Then it hit my mind like a grenade: the battle against fear and shame isn't external. The battle is fought in the eight inches between my ears. This realization changed everything. The life I want is sitting right there waiting to be taken once I eliminate fear and shame. I have to *decide* to take it, *decide* to build it, and *decide* to launch it.

> *Danger is very real, but fear is a choice.*[16]
> WILL SMITH AS CYPHER RAIGE IN *AFTER EARTH*

Everyone else is waiting around for life and success to be dropped into their laps, but as Abraham Lincoln aptly said, "The best way to predict your future is to create it." Right now, reading this page can be your turning point. It won't take years of counseling and years of healing. Those things are important, but I'd rather focus my time and energy on where I'm going and who I'm becoming than on where I've been. The common denominator in all our relationships, jobs, and circumstances is *us*.

Everyone talks about which wolves you will feed today. I say, remove the wolves. Life is about freedom in our true selves, not the management of our false selves. Life has to move away from constantly being in a mode of maintenance and move into abundant, thriving, and impactful living. We have become professional hamster-wheel builders of false identities because we have let fear take over. These wheels motivate us to keep moving, but we don't gain any value or purpose. We then start to resent everything around us wondering why our life isn't what we hoped it would be; and when we can't figure it out, we blame everyone else. This puts us on a mental island, and we look for ways to numb ourselves to drown out the pain and sorrow of the loss of our true self. I was a pro at this cycle, but I recognized that I have the ability to choose a different path and a different life.

We know the abundant life of living in the true self exists because we see others do it. Maybe we think it's because they have money or were brought up differently, but these excuses we make are precisely the battle. The fear that we are not able to achieve these things causes the excuses. The hope I have been convinced of is that God, through His Spirit, provided me the key to this battle. Even though fear is present and will persist until we die, we have a choice to buy into it and feed it, or we can silence it by not giving it power. Once I knew fear could be removed, it changed my life. I traded my team uniform and moved from the defense to the offense.

I became more aware of what was happening around me in my early 20s. As with most people in their 20s, we think about the way the world works, the people in it, our family, and how we will get over *there* from where we are standing *now*. It's easier for some than for others. I took a family assessment: both of my grandfathers worked the same job for thirty-six years. They were a part of the manufacturing age of factories, bosses, and careers. My parents' baby boomer generation was not very inclined toward entrepreneurship, though they were both creatives (thank goodness), and they lived in art and design. How was I going to approach life differently so that I could achieve my goals?

My generation was different. It was the technology and "anything goes" generation, though there was still an underlying theme of needing a traditional education to be successful. As I grew up, people were always talking about where you were going to go to college and to graduate with a master's degree in art and design. This fear, I can tell you, paralyzed me. I hated school even during my elementary years. I barely made it and was haunted by the belief that unless I had a piece of paper from an art school, I wasn't going to make it in life, would not be able to make a good income, or be able to support a family. I would only be able to live in a warehouse eating beans out of a can. Seriously, this fear pattern stuck with me for a long time.

Little did I realize that my thinking was way off. Too often I chose to believe what the world was offering. Now I appreciate that everyone is different, and there are an infinite number of paths to take. Their parents might have attended Yale, so they also went to Yale, but everyone is different and possesses different gifts. I graduated high school with no money, no job, and all I knew was that I loved creativity and doing my own thing.

How then does that kid end up thirty years later with a wife and two children working with and even consulting Fortune 500 companies? It started the day I chose to change my thinking. If you are going be hunting the enemy that has held you back, you need to uncover the dominating beliefs about yourself so that you can make better choices that lead you away from these misbeliefs.

I am a firm believer that my choices determine my outcomes. As I spent time analyzing this subject, I realized that we are all bound by some common limiting factors no matter when we were born or how we were raised. These four main points are time, unique gifts and talents, relationships, and the choices we make. I believe that narrowing these factors to just four points will narrow your focus to most effectively fight the battle against your false self.

You and I are both dealing with approximately the same amount of time given a normal human life span. You and I both have in common relationships, meaning we all have other people around us. You and I both have something we are able to do; this could be a specific talent or building a home or whatever skill you've developed. Here's the clincher: The one thing we have unlimited capacity for, and no ceiling on, is the power of making choices. We get to choose what we want when we want. We can alter our lives the moment we realize that our choices are our own. If you want to build a rocket ship and a castle, do it. It starts with deciding to do it and then taking action.

You've heard the phrase, "Life is what you make it." It's true. Once I realized the power of my choices, I started looking at my life on paper like a blueprint and began designing my dream days, my dream weeks, and so on. It became fun and exciting. I could literally feel myself leaving the status quo in the dust. Yes, there were a lot of unknowns, but the unknowns far outweighed the regret of staying stuck. What has kept you from designing your life the way you want it? When was the last time you dreamed? Have you been granted and given the permission to dream? I'm encouraging you to let go and open yourself up to this. Remember, we as humans all face the same challenge: We have to manage time, talents, money, and relationships. *How* we each manage our lives is what makes the difference.

Let's use Walt Disney as an example. One day he's sitting on a bench watching his daughters on a merry-go-round in a park. The next thing you know, he's sitting on his own park bench in Disneyland watching millions of people ride his own merry-go-round. He was dealing with time, he had a passion more than a gift, and he aligned his relationships with his passions. His choices are what really made the difference. He chose to not just dream, but he chose to take action and start asking, building, and launching. These choices were the key. Disney, as we know it, started with the simple thought of "what if?"

Walt Disney, based on his upbringing and the environment around him, would measure the choices he was about to make against the enemy of himself, his past, and the relationship between him and the culture he was living in. He assessed them all and was determined to build his life regardless of his limitations—not just for himself, but he used this gift of vision for the benefit of others. Talk about a fearhunter! Imagine the amount of fear, self-doubt, and self-talk that Walt Disney encountered in his life. Imagine all of the decisions, the bankers, the doubters, the haters—yet he chose to follow his calling and take risks.

Let's get one thing straight: Walt Disney recognized the gravity and importance of time. Most people live as if they will never run out of time. In reality, this mentality leads to spending or wasting time and not investing it. Like Walt and other visionaries, I realized at a young age that time is limited, and in order to live a life worth living, I had to understand the gravity of time. For example, to create a painting requires the artist to be physically present. To make money requires that the paintings sell. To make money again, he needs to make another one. The artist has two choices: make reproductions or hire more artists.

Walt realized that in order to create his vision while he was on this earth, he needed to leverage the relationships around him to create more of his vision in a faster, wider scope to gain as much traction during his limited time on earth. That is why he leveraged his home mortgage and everything he had to start building his dream. Now you realize why he hired artists to draw the animations, designers to build the parks, and teams to help execute the TV shows. Could he draw? Yes. Did he have an impressive education that qualified and gave him permission to accomplish all he did? No. The bottom line is that he chose to make it happen. He realized that he had time, relationships, unique abilities, and choices. How he boldly and wisely chose to use his time, talent, and relationships is what made him successful. Walt is one of the best examples of a fearhunter. He knew that the outcome far outweighed the criticism, debt, risk, failure, and exhaustion. Like Walt, I'd rather go to bed a failure than go to bed with regret.

Lack of time is one of the biggest motivators to hunting fear. If we are being defeated by fear, it robs our precious time on earth that we can't get back. The sooner we remove the fears, shame, and doubts, the sooner we can be available for making wise and healthy choices, producing fruit in our lives. The battleground is fought in our mind and the choices we make. Choose to get control of your life and decide what the output is going to be.

ENEMY BATTLEGROUND: THE POWER OF CHOICE

#HUNTING TARGETS

1. When it comes to your choices in life, what voice do you hear in your head? Yours? Your parents? The culture and others?

2. On a scale of 1-10 (10 being "absolutely"), would you say your choices are based on you *living* your life?

3. If money wasn't an object and you had $50 million in the bank, would you be bolder in your choices or the same?

4. What do you need in order to have freedom in your choices? What's holding you back? Write it down.

5. Based on your answer to #4, what is needed for you to remove what stands in your way so that you can get freedom? How do you plan to overcome these and when? Make a deadline and tackle one at a time. This could be a phone call, an email, or simply starting a new discipline or habit.

PART TWO

ENTER THE PIT:
VISIT THE NIGHTMARE, RESCUE
THE CHILD WITHIN, AND DEFEAT
THE ENEMY

#CHAPTER 8

A RADICAL NEW LIFE: BECOME A FEARHUNTER

God is our refuge and strength, a very present help in trouble. Therefore we will not fear though the earth gives way, though the mountains be moved into the heart of the sea, though its waters roar and foam, though the mountains tremble at its swelling.
PSALM 46:1–3 (ESV)

People who ask confidently get more than those who are hesitant and uncertain. Now that you've figured out what you want to ask for, do it with certainty, boldness and confidence. Don't be shy or feel intimidated by the experience. You may face some unexpected criticism, but be prepared for it with confidence.[17]

JACK CANFIELD, MOTIVATIONAL SPEAKER, AUTHOR

I think naturally if you're an actor, there's a high level of assertiveness that you need to have to survive this business. There's boldness in being assertive, and there's strength and confidence.[18]

BRYAN CRANSTON, ACTOR (WALTER WHITE, *BREAKING BAD*)

WHEN I WAS A KID, I REMEMBER WATCHING SYLVESTER Stallone in the movie, *Rambo*. It's an incredible movie about an ex-military guy who is chased down by the police. At one point in the story, he receives a massive laceration on his arm and performs surgery on himself. He pulls out a needle and thread and begins to sew up the wound without any anesthetic. It was incredible. I remember watching with friends, saying, "Dude! That guy is crazy!" Rambo's boldness was what I wanted for my life. I wanted to be able to live with an attitude that even if life cuts me and I get knocked down, I get back up and throw a right hook.

Most of us are not living in this kind of boldness. Instead, fears, like the ones we have explored, reveal the symptoms of what we have fabricated to fill a void in our hearts. We have filled our hearts with false identities, false passions, and false ways of living out of fear that we would be left vulnerable and subject to getting hurt. We have become cranky, frustrated adults, and we don't understand why. We have made agreements with the lies generated by our family of origin, and we have taken that record and played it on the record player of our future. We believe that these circumstances determine how our lives will always be, so we lie to ourselves and say, "Just deal with it." I've got great news. You don't have to.

Life on the offense is such a radical paradigm shift that it is beyond words. If you have been paralyzed by fears, anxiety, and stress, my prayer is that you can live with hope and operate from an assured place of rest. This transformation is going to require action and some digging on your part. It's going to get dirty, and it's going to be you threading a needle to sew yourself up. The great thing is that you aren't alone in this.

I was spending most of my days combating the fact that fear was fully present in my daily decisions and challenges. It grew even worse as I moved closer to living my calling. The more I became authentic and truthful about what I wanted out of life, the more fear I battled. I then began a journey of searching for the cause of my fear instead of the symptoms. That's when I learned about shame. Fear was the representative of shame, but shame was the root cause. I am a performance-based person, so shame was my default. Shame says, "You are who you are based on what you do." A majority of the fears I faced daily were based on letting others down. I worried that God was mad at me, or that I wouldn't receive God's love unless I performed. Business deals were motivated in performing out of shame rather than enjoying the opportunity to work with a client. I would perform to get approval from the client in order to receive connection, love, money, and support. Fear of confrontation and letting people down was rooted in shame based on my performance. The moment I began to recognize and eliminate the shame, the fears were removed.

For some reading this, life has been lived on the sidelines or even tailgating in the parking lot.

You wish to be out on the field where the action is, but it has been tough to get out of the funk. Trust me, I understand. That's where I was.

Imagine living a life in which regardless of how crazy or chaotic things are, you can be on the offense and at peace. Imagine relationships with others not driven by fear and performance. Imagine not running your day based on the fear of what others think of you. Imagine the upbringing you had not being what defines you. Imagine the traumas and nightmares and the past being the greatest blessing of how God wants to use you today. Imagine walking boldly in your own skin, taking complete ownership and excitement in the joy of who you are, who you were designed to be, and how you are to live out your life. Sound like a pipe dream or a mirage? It's not. It's true. I, as well as others, have escaped the prison of the false self and have never looked back.

The goal for us is to not live life in the realm of being a reactor and a victim. It's about being in the driver's seat and in control of our thoughts and actions. Becoming a fearhunter means that we become the hunter rather than the hunted. We can either be plagued by fear, or we can eliminate it. What I'm describing is a decision and a mindset followed by a lifestyle.

READY ... AIM, AIM, AIM, AIM ... THE STRATEGY AND ACTION PLAN

Have you ever talked with a dreamer? I'm talking about the ones who are constantly in the mode of dreaming with no action. I believe that once we finally get the gumption to dream big, fear of failure crops up, and we stay in a dreaming mode. We will go in depth on how to remove fear and shame, but it's key to realize that this change doesn't just happen. You don't work out once at a gym and then get buff by just thinking about it. You repeat it. The same goes for life. You can't stay in the dream stage concerning the life that you want to live; you must begin to build it one small step at a time. Tackle one small goal that fits into a series of goals that make up the larger sum of your dream life. Getting there will require unclogging the drain of your mind and the paradigms that block it.

Your brain is the epicenter of your choices. I've said many times that I'd rather deal with failure than regret. The fact that you are taking action by reading this book is a great step. I want to urge you to not just put this on the shelf as a trophy of more knowledge. We read books and acquire knowledge, but it doesn't turn into wisdom until we act on it. When we act on truth and wisdom, we see and experience the fruit. The work that lies ahead of you will require action. You will need to choose action. Don't just think about it; do it!

Below you will find an outline of the steps we will walk through to take you from the defense to the offense, from the hunted to the hunter. Each step will be detailed in the chapters to follow.

Step 1—Make the choice to change and fight fear.

Step 2—Get your heart right—pursue discovering the heart of God.

Step 3—Free up poorly used mental space.

Step 4—Measure your self-worth by God's standards.

Step 5—Take action by identifying false friends.

Step 6—Take action by going back to the identity created in traumatic childhood events and showing compassion and acceptance to the child.

Step 7—Live boldly in your true identity in authority, partnering with God.

As we learned before, the fear of letting others down, the fear of confrontation, and the fear of failure are all rooted in self—the false self. In order to remove the false self and its byproduct of fear, we are required to get to the root cause. Look at it this way: the fears we deal with on a daily basis and the self-talk in our heads are the symptoms. Most doctors and therapists make a great living dealing with and managing the symptoms. They might help make the self-talk a little quieter, but my goal is to remove the problem entirely. It can happen. You just have to be willing to dive deep. Here is one of the most important truths to remember in the process of what's to come in the next few chapters: We are looking to heal your past events. The traumas, the pain, the things that were your worst nightmares are not the issue. *The issue is your heart.*

> *"And you will know the truth, and the truth will set you free."*
>
> JOHN THE BELOVED (JOHN 8:32, NLT)

So as we journey into these next few chapters, remember that we aren't hunting to quiet symptoms or deal with past situations. We aren't using Band-Aids to cover up and manage the pain or bleeding. We are diving back into our past to visit the child within to deal with his or her heart. You might have terrifying nightmares and horrible memories, but remember that the worst nightmares and the fears of our past hold the keys to our freedom, our true selves, and to authentic living. If we have safety and we are rooted in truth, we will accomplish our goals.

#HUNTING TARGETS

1. I want to encourage you to not be a ready aim thinker. What would life look like if you fired the weapon?

2. In what areas of your life do you feel like you are analyzing things to death out of fear?

3. What is stopping you from taking action?

#CHAPTER 9

LOVE: THE HEART OF THE MATTER

*Our inclination is to show our Lord only what we feel
comfortable with. But the more we dare to reveal our whole
trembling self to him, the more we will be able to sense that
his love, which is perfect love, casts out all our fears.*[19]

HENRI NOUWEN, PROFESSOR AT YALE, HARVARD, NOTRE DAME,
CATHOLIC PRIEST

*Your identity as a child of God means that you are valuable
and loved regardless of what you do.*

NOAH

DURING THE 1990S, I LIVED AS A VICTIM IN FULL FORCE. I believed that my past defined who I was. I believed that my parents' history was my future and that I was living in a way that wasn't authentic. It wasn't until later that I realized I had to get my heart fixed. If you want to attain the freedom that we have been discussing, there is a root issue that needs to be addressed for true healing and removal of fear. Because our hearts are the epicenter of where past traumas and wounds stay locked as memories, and these memories can determine our daily decisions, it is essential to repair our hearts as the second step in our fear hunting process.

Put simply, we have to discover who has control of our hearts. There are only three options: ourselves, others, or God, our Creator. This discovery is paramount because if others are ruling our hearts, then our lives aren't our own. We become codependent and wear ourselves out to perform and win approval from coworkers, family, friends, or significant others. It's exhausting. We feel empty and invisible because shame, measured by our performance, defines us. The more we do, the more we get (connection and love). All the praise in the world won't cure the emptiness we feel because it isn't connecting with the right source—our heart.

Controlling our own hearts is a lonely dead-end street. I can speak to this personally. I was the guy spending most of my time in the self-help department of the bookstore looking for any tool or resource to repair and equip myself. I did everything to get educated on how to be productive and to live efficiently. The problem was that I was working on the *how* and not the *why* or *who*. I cared about how to be more productive and efficient, but not about who or why I was motivated to be better. I came to realize that a life and heart run by myself will burn a person out quickly. It's the hamster-wheel approach of doing life that goes nowhere. It's heading from California to New York on a journey with no map and no plan. In essence, taking the journey of life alone is solitary confinement and a missed opportunity to experience God's intended plan for collaboration with others and with His abundance.

The why and the who are the two main motivation questions that we should constantly be asking when it comes to our hearts. When we meet someone new at a restaurant or dinner party, they always ask, "So, what do you do?" They never ask who you do it for or why you do it because our culture doesn't usually think this way. I want to save you a ton of time and effort and to encourage you to turn from *uncritically* adapting to the general culture of the world that often does not ask these critical questions of motivation. If you really want to see your life take shape, get in tune with discovering the heart of God. I know it might be a different approach to what you have learned or heard, but I personally found my heart in His.

Removing fear and shame from your life requires love and compassion. The only way this process can work is with true love. So how do we possess this love? How does it work? It starts with an invitation. I believe that God continually pursues a relationship with man and He is after man's heart. Little did I know that God had been pursuing my heart during this whole journey. I believe that the entire purpose for our existence is to be in relationship. You've heard people say that there is a God-sized hole in each person's heart that only God can fill. I believe this is true, and through this process, I have discovered and experienced a love like no other. If you understand the following powerful concepts, they have the potential to change your life forever.

We can never earn God's love because it's a gift. This is the definition of perfect love. It can't be earned; it is only given in grace. The moment we enter into a relationship with God, we are immersed into His glorious grace. We are protected, adopted, and bought with the sacrifice of God's Son to live with Him for eternity. There's nothing we can do or say to lose that position with Him once we say yes to this relational bond. The Scriptures describe this relationship with Christ as a marriage, and He will not break His vows, even when we are faithless. Though our bodies waste away, our hearts are constantly growing in Him and expanding in love. It just keeps getting better.

As you are about to hunt down your own heart, realize that your heart has been hunted since the day you were born. God has been in pursuit of your heart from day one, wanting to talk with you, love you, and spend time with you. He loves you far more than you could ever imagine. In order to be ready to remove fear and shame and to dive into past memories to disarm the bombs, your heart has to be ready and include the ultimate weapon—*perfect* love and compassion, found only in Jesus Christ. He is pumped to do life with you. Life isn't meant to be done alone. This is why you were created—for community with Him.

You may be reading this and not know a thing about God. Perhaps you know Him but have not been communicating with Him for a while. That's okay. What matters to Him most is that you are aware of His presence and the truth that He loves you and has already forgiven you. Your guilt and shame, as well as your wrongdoing, are nailed to that cross. Knowing this is key to the next few chapters because, without Him, full removal can't happen.

The greatest news is that you are taking steps toward changing your life and choices forever. This soul work is the greatest discovery and investment that you can make, and it will have *forever* implications. There have been so many of God's fingerprints on my journey that they are too abundant to count—even before I made the choice to live for Him. I believe some of these relationships and circumstances literally took a miracle to happen. More than luck, it took an act of God for some of them to be accomplished. As you embark on this journey with God, you will have your heart and identity invaded by love. It might be the first time you have ever felt safe or loved without condition. Trust me, you are loved. You matter to Him, and you are not alone.

As you take this second step in the fear hunting process, I encourage you to simply get quiet to talk with God. Start with a peaceful place. It could be right where you are sitting. You could be on a plane, listening to this on a bike ride, or traveling in your car. You are about to do some serious business to remove fear and shame from your life, and I believe that you can't completely remove fear through self-will alone. The key ingredient for full removal is perfect love and compassion. I would pray something like this:

God, I come to You to surrender myself to be immersed in Your love. I'm tired of trying to manage my fear, guilt, and shame. I believe You love me. I accept the gift of love that You gave to me through Your Son, Jesus. I believe that He died and was raised to conquer death, defeat sin, and has overcome and forgiven all of my wrongdoing.

I ask You to live in my heart, to take control of my life, and renew me to be who You've created me to be. Align my will with Yours and provide me with the wisdom to follow You and to discover Your heart. Cleanse me and make me whole. As I address my fears and shame, help me see Your perfect love and compassion for me. Guide me and help me undo that which holds me back. Thank You for loving me. I receive Your love. Help me to see myself as You see me. Reveal to me my true identity in Your love. I choose You. Amen.

Know and *practice* believing that you are a child of God and you are celebrated by Him!

God is perfect love. He is the truth and the truth will set you free. Complete removal of your fears and shame is possible because of Him. Unconditional love from God was hard for me to embrace because I was used to experiencing shame. And shame tells us that our worth as humans is based on our performance. This is the message that empowered the lies in my life: If I do well, He will love me and provide for me. If I make bad choices, He won't love me; I'll be cut off from connection and love. As a child of God, your heart and identity have changed. You are loved unconditionally. Remember this throughout your life: Your identity as a child of God means that you are valuable and loved regardless of what you do.

#HUNTING TARGETS

1. What have been your past messages about God? Write them out.

2. Do you see God as a loving Father who cares about you and is interested in you?

3. Do you project the character of your earthly father on to your view and feeling of God?

4. List the wrongdoings that come to mind as the worst nightmares, biggest secrets, and most terrible things you hate about yourself. Then burn them. As you burn that paper (in a safe place), pray to God and imagine nailing them to the cross as He is taking them and forgiving them. He removes your sin as far as the east is from the west. They are gone and forgotten. You are forgiven. Let go.

5. After burning the list, write out at least ten things you are grateful for that come to mind. You are free. You have just been released from a prison in your beliefs and mind and have just been submerged in a sea of love and truth. Write out how you feel. You are a prince or a princess and a priceless gift in God's eyes. He doesn't make mistakes. You are perfect in His eyes, and He is so proud of you for making these bold moves toward intimacy with Him. Crawl up in His lap; let Him hold you and love you. You've traveled a long road. He wants to do life with you every minute moving forward.

#CHAPTER 10

MENTAL HOARDING: HOLDING ON TO LIES AND FALSE SELF-IDENTITIES

A man who is "of sound mind" is one who keeps the inner madman under lock and key.[20]

PAUL VALÉRY, PHILOSOPHER, AUTHOR, POET

The ego is only an illusion, but a very influential one. Letting the ego-illusion become your identity can prevent you from knowing your true self. Ego, the false idea of believing that you are what you have or what you do, is a backwards way of assessing and living life.[21]

DR. WAYNE DYER, *NEW YORK TIMES* BEST-SELLING AUTHOR

MENTAL HOARDING: HOLDING ON TO LIES AND FALSE SELF-IDENTITIES

OUR BATTLE IS NOT EXTERNAL; IT IS AN INTERNAL BATTLE fought between our true selves and the enemy of fear and shame on the battleground of our mind. I want you to think of your mind like a computer, which runs best when the memory isn't full. Our brains and creativity run best when we aren't tapped out managing emotions and trying to control chaotic thinking. We have to free up the space currently taken up by the management of fear and shame in order to live powerful lives.

For God has not given us a spirit of fear and timidity, but of power, love, and self-discipline.

PAUL THE APOSTLE (2 TIMOTHY 1:7, NLT)

One translation of this verse says, "and a sound mind." This is one gift that I craved—a sound mind, the control center, the control room of my thinking and beliefs. Inside this mind lay the truth of God's Word, and the enemy was working overtime to corrupt my thinking in order to gain control and influence over my choices.

For our struggle is not against flesh and blood, but against the rulers, against the powers, against the world forces of this darkness, against the spiritual forces of wickedness in the heavenly places.

PAUL THE APOSTLE (EPHESIANS 6:12)

Therefore if anyone is in Christ, he is a new creature; the old things passed away; behold, new things have come.

PAUL THE APOSTLE (2 CORINTHIANS 5:17)

How badly do you desire freedom? Being comfortable in your own skin? Living life on purpose rather than managing and coping? We have a life of abundance that is beyond measure available to us through our Creator. What keeps us from our true self and abundant living are the agreements we make with lies, shame, and fear. We act as if we are the victim of these plagues, but in fact, we are the ones who agree with them and allow them in. We choose them. If we can take a moment to examine and drill down into our fears, lies, and shame, we can remove these toxic elements that are hindering our lives. We can step into the truth and reality of who we are and who we were created to be.

The apostle Paul spoke of being transformed by the renewing of our mind. The key to learning new behaviors and habits is repetition. You become what you mentally digest. If you want to put on the truth muscle, you'll need to hit the mental gym often.

My routine starts in the morning, typically in the early hours before anyone in my family is up. I spend time in the Bible, reading wisdom, and committing Scripture to memory. I read powerful affirmations out loud, many of which are contained in this book. These affirmations aren't just for me; they are for everyone. Read these to yourself: I am a child of God, a co-heir of Christ. I am clothed in righteousness. I am safe in the shadow of my Father. He has plans for me that reach beyond anything I can imagine. I am a warrior in His army. He sees me as an amazing masterpiece that He created. I am here on purpose. My life has a plan and it's done in partnership with my Father. I am fearfully and wonderfully made in His eyes. God is pursuing me every day with His love even if I am not pursuing Him. I have what it takes to live an impactful life and have been equipped with every heavenly resource needed to carry out my calling. I am loved beyond measure.

I then spend time addressing my inner child, which means I am talking to my heart. I literally talk out loud to my heart. I ask my heart, "Hey buddy, what do you need? How are you feeling today? How can I help? What would you like to do? What desires do you have?"

I then spend time concentrating on God's presence through the Holy Spirit, knowing He is in the room. I seek His heart as if I were talking to a close friend sitting next to me. Where is His heart? How can I get to know Him better? I use Scripture to remember all He has done for me. I think of His character and how I can recognize His love. We talk.

One of the best strategies that has brought massive healing in my life is having a "place" that I can visualize where God and I hang out. For me, it is an actual beach that I go to, but I can also go to that place in my head in prayer. This provides a supernatural focus for me.

I am extremely intentional in my routine because I know that freedom isn't cheap. What did it cost? It cost God sacrificing the life of His only Son that we might have eternal hope and love with Him. This sacrifice is the key to providing us true freedom, from ourselves and from the stronghold of the world. Once you believe this truth, the key is moving to a sense of knowing this truth. Knowledge doesn't take the form of wisdom until it is put into action and experienced. If you truly want freedom, it is going to require some serious action and digging on your part. Here's the good news—the moment you start to dig, your Creator and His angels stand beside you cheering for you, excited about the release of your true self, a new identity, and new assignments.

Life is too short to spend our time managing self, false identities, and baggage from the past. Once we are set free, we contain the mental capacity to live in our authentic, true self, producing eternal results.

STUFFED ANIMALS AND HARD DRIVES

I recently saw a dilapidated old car on the side of the road. The person inside looked lost and defeated. The back seat was packed with faded stuffed animals to the point where you couldn't see out of the car. It was as if the car was a storage unit. Looking at this situation gave me a feeling of anxiety and served as a physical representation of what happens in people's mental lives. People too often allow issues, traumas, and baggage to accumulate in their lives, and the emotional congestion becomes a new norm. This congestion can manifest in weight gain, health issues, financial trouble, bad habits, fears, and poor relationships.

I believe we can clean up the exterior of our lives with a well-managed lifestyle and at the same time, we can leave the inside of our soul unfinished, dirty, clogged, and full of faded stuffed animals. We can hang on to so many burdens that we can't see out of the windshield, let alone the rear of the car. Leaving fears, lies, and shame unaddressed will accumulate in your mind and impair you as you grow older. Fear and shame take root when we are children and can continue to build through our formative years. Our soul and spirit can only hold so much. This emotional hoarding is another issue to manage, making poor use of our mental space. Externally, we may have an amazing balanced and clean life with family, career, community, and church, yet inside a serious infestation is taking place. It appears we are living well, but in fact, our souls are corrupt.

CHOOSING FALSE FRIENDS INSTEAD OF SELF-AWARENESS

Why do we allow this hoarding? I believe that we all look for comfort, connection, and security in external things. It's in our nature. One problem with seeking these comforts is that over time we become increasingly unaware of what we are hoarding. In previous chapters, I quoted John 8:32, "You shall know the truth, and the truth shall make you free" (NKJV). What is the truth? I believe that the truth is God's Word, His wisdom, and His will, and that all truth ultimately belongs to God.

Now here is my favorite question: Who is the truth? In the above verse, Jesus says, "I am the truth." Now read the verse again, "You shall know (Jesus), and (Jesus) shall set you free." It's one thing for us to have knowledge of the truth, and it's another thing for us to "know" the Person of truth. Many people don't know that there is a way out of this mental and spiritual prison. Jesus Christ is the key to this freedom, this transformation and release of your true self. Why? Because He created you. Through Him, we can know and receive our true identities and trade in the false friends and everything else we've hoarded: our past, our fears, and our shame.

GYM MEMBERSHIPS AND THE FLOATING GUY IN MUSCLE PANTS

Acquire wisdom! Acquire understanding! Do not forget nor turn away from the words of my mouth.
KING SOLOMON (PROVERBS 4:5)

I used to visit a gym near my office. It was always interesting to watch the different forms of people who attended. As I was on the stair climber, I would see these older guys float into the gym. They wore old-school muscle shirts with baggy pants and would spend 90 percent of their time walking around the gym, talking to friends. They had a membership but didn't really use the membership for its benefit. What use is it to have a membership to a gym when you have no idea what to do when you get there? Do you set out to lose weight with no guidance or way to do it? Likewise, some people have a membership in God's kingdom and have never used it. Human nature defaults to laziness and inaction. It takes discipline, self-awareness, and action to overcome this in all areas of life. In the same way, wisdom can be similarly mishandled.

EMOTIONAL AND SPIRITUAL VOMITING EARN THE REWARDS AT THE END OF THIS JOURNEY

If this book is Mt. Everest and you have decided to climb it with me, I would tell you that we are pulling up to base camp one. We have a couple of stages left to go, but the next stage is crucial. What lies ahead is an emotional vomit for your soul, heart, and spirit that will reveal the shame and fears within you that can be eliminated. As we begin to take this climb, let's realize that elimination is our goal and the prize is at the summit: freedom and a life of peace. Let me explain the reward and prize a bit.

The summit and the prize for me weren't just elimination of fear and shame. I wanted more.

That's why I was willing to allow God to prune my life in order to grow more fruit. When God prunes your life, learn to lean into the process though it may be painful at the moment. The prize is freedom to operate in your calling and unique design. You are one of a kind and have been created to do amazing things here on earth. That freedom is a peace that surpasses all understanding.

And the peace of God, which transcends all understanding,
will guard your hearts and your minds in Christ Jesus.
PAUL THE APOSTLE (PHILIPPIANS 4:7, NIV)

Remember, what we are after here is transformation

And do not be conformed to this world, but be transformed
by the renewing of your mind, so that you may prove what
the will of God is, that which is good and acceptable and
perfect.
PAUL THE APOSTLE (ROMANS 12:2)

We aren't here to become happy. Happiness is based on circumstances. True happiness comes from knowing the truth of who you are, who you are becoming and who you are living for. That is a joy that never runs out. We are here to produce fruit that will be taken with us eternally. As Tim

Ferriss has said, "Happiness can be purchased with a bottle of wine."[22] The end goal is knowing the truth and doing it. It's that simple. Reaching the summit has little to do with money and possessions. It's all about freedom and living in your calling.

WILL YOU HURL ON THE ROLLER COASTER?

In the next chapters, we will start to eliminate and go into some depths that you might not have ever explored. There might be gross, disturbing memories and scary stuff you will encounter, but this journey is beyond worth it. Anxiety and panic attacks have been a part of my life and I truly understand these feelings. Nothing is better than traumas being dealt with and behind us. Fear hunting is an action on ourselves, on the child within us that needs rescuing. It's a battle for your future and for your soul. Expect interference and expect hidden emotions to show up during the remainder of the book. It will be a roller coaster of a ride. You might hate the book and throw it across the room. You might cry. You might puke and you might feel that the process is forced. You might even be embarrassed, so let me prepare you—this is a war and you're going to win. You're the hero/heroine, and you will plant your flag in the summit and take selfies to show everyone (maybe you should take a "before" selfie now and then take one after you've reached the summit).

Wouldn't it be amazing to wake up knowing that you are doing exactly what you are supposed to be doing and how you are supposed to be doing it? Let's emotionally be willing to vomit and purge the false self because it will yield a truer identity in Christ. You are fearfully and wonderfully made. Let's start the next stage of the climb. Are you with me?

#HUNTING TARGETS

1. Where in your internal life are you hoarding lies?

2. What self-talk do you listen to daily? Is it about your looks, your weight, your actions, your abilities, or something else?

3. Do you believe you have been living as a poser or a fraud?

4. If you told the truth about yourself, what might people find out? What would happen if they did?

5. How many moments of each day do you find that you are living as your true self?

6. If you go through this book to remove your false identities, what do freedom and peace look like in your life?

#CHAPTER 11

THE SHAME GAME

The greater the obstacle, the more glory in overcoming it.[23]

MOLIERE, FRENCH PLAYWRIGHT

FOR THE LAST THIRTY-SEVEN YEARS, I HAVE STRUGGLED with a nagging feeling that something bad was about to happen to me because I had unknowingly done something wrong and was going to be found out. I had feelings of "being bad" or of low self-worth even thought I hadn't done anything wrong. It seriously was driving me nuts. I couldn't shake it. The crazy thing was that on the outside, everything was fantastic. I had my dream life with my family, and everything seemed to be flowing well.

I remember one day waking up early to go work out around five in the morning to get quiet, read, pray, and unpack the day. I had these thoughts and feelings nagging and plaguing my mind. The best way to describe them was feeling bad, like a kid who's not accepted and overcome with shame. For years I thought it was guilt. For a while, I thought it was depression or just a season, but it kept persisting and felt constant. I kept asking myself, "How can I be feeling like this or having thoughts like this with all the great things happening?" I then began to read books that talked about leaders and successful people not feeling worth the success they had achieved. That idea resonated, but there was still more.

I started thinking about my past and realized that because of my upbringing, I would earn love, favor, and connection by doing and performing. Everything I did was driven by performance. My mantra was: If I do good, then I am good; if I do bad, then I am bad. For example, I would strive for an impressive performance with my youth pastors. I loved them and appreciated them. I wanted their approval and for them to want me around. Whenever I was with them, the driving force behind my choices became to impress them and perform for them. I felt, even as an adult, that if I was a good boy, I was going to get connection and love. So in light of this upbringing and my continued struggles, I reached back into my earliest memories of fear and shame to discover that the key to my freedom was sitting in my worst nightmares as a child.

At first, I tried to eliminate these bad feelings from my life by praying against them as fear and guilt. I had the right weapon but the wrong target. The target wasn't guilt or fear. The target was shame because my whole self-worth was based on performance.

I believe generalized fear is the symptom of a root cause. Fear isn't real. The events, situations, and outcomes that it conjures are imagined. The events of my past birthed fears that became my false friends and false identities. Over the course of my adult life, I made agreements, unconsciously, that snowballed into a lifestyle of managing symptoms. I was irritable, punchy in my attitude and spirit, and didn't feel good enough, ever. I felt alone even with a family and a lot of friends. I was frustrated. I also wanted more, but I couldn't get rid of the negative self-talk that told me I wasn't a "good boy." I had learned the art of beheading fears, but the queen bee was still in charge when I faced my largest fear—shame.

As I said, though this relationship with shame began when I was a child, it continued to manifest as an adult. As crazy as this sounds, in my earlier adult life, I would accept and unconsciously invite problematic people and relationships in that would keep me busy trying to meet unhealthy expectations, which then provided the shame of failure when they couldn't be met. This shame would then help me feel connected to my past and my parents. As sick as this sounds, we will make unhealthy choices in the present that link us back to the past as a connection to our old identities and a false sense of security—to a place that feels familiar and ironically comforting. Then, before we know it, our present and future are based on lies. I know, it's crazy; but it's true. If you look carefully at your life, you'll see how you've been following a similar pattern.

Shame's number one game is to keep us defining the worth of our life based on other people's perceptions and the self-talk we have in our heads. Shame is a measuring stick that is clothed in performance: *If I do or act in this way, I will receive love and connection. If I don't perform and behave well, I will lose what I have, so therefore, I will "do" out of fear.* Fear became my fuel and compulsion in life. The soul becomes frustrated when fear is its only motivation, especially because as adults, we know we aren't being true to ourselves.

Over the last year I've studied fear and learned steps and techniques to overcome it, but freedom came when I learned about the shame game. I learned that shame piggybacks on fear. As soon as this idea became obvious in my life, fear and shame both started to vanish. Remember, identity in shame says, "You are who you are based on what you do." Identity in God says, "You are who you are regardless of what you do." This outlook was so profound that it changed everything in my life.

In *The 4-Hour Work Week*, Tim Ferriss talks about how an idle mind left to itself will turn in on itself and create unnecessary problems. I agree. I find that my self-talk is a coping mechanism and comforting tactic that I created as a young boy to deal with stress and fear. Even though my self-talk was unhealthy, it was one of the few consistent things in my life. I longed for consistency in light of my parents' divorce and struggled with the constant feeling that I didn't belong. Just like my false friends—fear and shame—my self-talk was the voice that I heard when I agreed with lies. This pattern became so consistent that it made the shame feel more believable and true. So we can use our self-talk as a map in order to target our past shame. However, as we get older, this self-talk and dialogue become pests because we realize that they are keeping us from living. We end up managing them rather than thriving. Finding your past shames begins by listening to yourself in order to discover and eliminate negative self-talk. One of the greatest signposts of shame in your life is self-talk. If you're like me, you don't realize it's even happening.

The hunting targets on the following page are meant to help you begin to find moments of shame from your past that are still affecting you today. Keep these answers nearby as they are going to help in the coming chapters. The more you dig, the more revelations will arise in the coming days and hours. Be on the lookout, as your mundane daily tasks will evoke memories while you are in the discovery process. And don't dismiss the gross; that is to say, I remember when I went through this, the disturbing memories of my past and the things I had seen and witnessed held the keys to freedom. One of your main targets is to recognize the memory and the lie you tell yourself in your self-talk as a result of those unpleasant memories.

Once you start to get the hang of this process, the past shame issues will come down like dominoes, and your spirit will start to soar.

#HUNTING TARGETS

1. What situation(s) from your youth made you feel embarrassed?

2. What words from your youth, which someone said about you, do you continue to repeat in your head today?

3. What self-talk, myths, and lies do you keep hearing each day in your thoughts?

4. What are the themes or commonalities in these statements?

5. When do you remember adopting these statements in life? How old were you?

#CHAPTER 12

DISARMING BOMBS THROUGH COMPASSION

For you have not received a spirit of slavery leading to fear again, but you have received a spirit of adoption as sons by which we cry out, "Abba! Father!"

PAUL THE APOSTLE (ROMANS 8:15)

My mission in life is not merely to survive, but to thrive; and to do so with some passion, some compassion, some humor, and some style.[24]

MAYA ANGELOU, POET, CIVIL RIGHTS ACTIVIST

IF YOU HAVE MADE IT THIS FAR IN THE BOOK, YOU HAVE chosen to reach for a life of authenticity, free of fear and shame, by giving your heart to Jesus and uncovering the events in your life where shame took have taken in your heart, allowing your mind to be overrun by fear.

In order to heal and eliminate the shame of the past, I traveled back and healed the memory or the precipitating event that resulted in shame. The goal is to heal the child and his or her identity in the event. The target we are after, or the trauma, is what happened to our identities and hearts at the event. Whether it was sexual abuse, being embarrassed as a child in front of others, a parent walking out, a parent missing the school play, a lack of nurturance or other moments that defined your self-worth and identity as a child, these influential events have to be explored and the resulting identities healed in order to eliminate fear and shame. Remember, it's not necessarily the event that caused the issue; it's what happened to our heart in the event.

I had some events in my childhood that were traumatic. My focus for many years was forgiving the people who had wronged me. My goal was to try to make a bad situation better. That is a good place to start hunting, but it's not the complete picture. You will erase elements of the memory, but you won't annihilate and remove the core issue. The target to address is your heart and the condition of your heart in the trauma. The heart makes an agreement or a vow or goes into protection mode as a child when we are threatened or going to lose love. Let's see the process in action. Below are some examples of past traumas from my childhood that formed my identity:

It was a clear, bright, sunny afternoon. I was playing in a Little League game. We were running a pretty close game. I was at the bottom of the batting lineup. I was a so-so hitter and a better player in the field. I remember the sun was going down and the field was glowing in a golden sunset. As I was about to walk out of the dugout, my coach said, "Aim for the fence in the outfield." It was the typical saying, like, "Hey buddy, hit it out of the park." I remember the guys on my team being pretty cool. At that time in my life, being 11 years old, I wasn't really bullied. Life wasn't great, but it wasn't terrible. It just was.

As I stepped up to home plate, I dug in my feet. I was planning to hit this ball with everything I had. The bases were loaded and the other team sent in a relief pitcher. I had a feeling this kid was going to throw a curveball, so I moved way up in the batter's box to catch it early before it broke. The pitch came in. It was a curve ball. I remember hitting it with all I had.

I immediately started to run, but I looked to my left to see the ball going down the left field foul line high in the air. I was thinking, as was everyone else, that it was a foul ball. But this ball started to creep back into play in the air. Sometimes I wonder if an angel was in the air blowing that ball into fair territory because a ball usually fades left instead of breaking into the field. The left fielder watched it soar over his head. With a few inches to spare, this ball fell over the fence. The place went silent and then erupted. It was a grand slam! I remember running the bases laughing, and I couldn't believe the feeling. It was indescribable. The team mobbed me at the plate. My coach was laughing at what just happened, and we slaughtered the other team that day.

After the initial excitement, I realized that my dad wasn't around. I couldn't find him anywhere in the crowd or along the fence. Innings later he poked his head into the dugout holding the ball, although he had just arrived at the field. I don't even remember what he said because I couldn't believe that he had missed my grand slam. I felt invisible that day. It wouldn't have mattered if the whole world had shown up. My value wasn't in them; it was in my caretaker, my dad. His was the one opinion that mattered. I didn't feel valued, noticed, or seen.

The baseball game was an epicenter of shame for me. From that memory, I created multiple vows. These included, "I never want to be like my dad," or "I'll prove myself," or "I'll show the world and be seen by everyone." I then operated life from lies and misbeliefs. These vows weren't healthy as they ruled my thinking and formed my identity. Only later on was I able to see my dad in this moment, not as the villain or trauma. I was able to forgive him, myself, and the event. If we desire removal and freedom, it requires seeing the traumas and events through truth. If we continue to view traumas in our life through bruised ego, selfish pride, and through the immature emotional lens we had when the trauma happened, we will continue to see life as a victim rather than to live in freedom and true identity.

The game and the grand slam weren't the event that needed to be healed. It was my identity in that moment that needed to be redeemed. I prayed to go to this boy and give him what he really needed that day. I met that kid in the dugout and I talked to him. Because I am an adult now, I have the maturity to process this tough event and help young Noah through it. I went up to little Noah in the dugout and told him, "Now that was a hit!!! You ripped the cover off that ball! I'm so proud of you! I saw the whole thing! You're amazing kid! Will you sign the ball for me? Let's go celebrate after the game." I then turned to the crowd and beamed with pride. This prayer and going back to that memory in order to give myself what I needed were profound. This was possible because I saw myself as God sees me: in truth, the real me, the warrior, the strong kid, the grand-slam hitter.

In another of my prayer healing sessions, I was taken back to when I was 11 years old. I had been kicked out of an art contest at my school because they thought that my entry was too advanced and that my dad had drawn it and I was disqualified. Man, that one stung. That memory and trauma became the beginning recipe for a cocktail that I would mix to make shame my caretaker. I used shame as a mechanism to cope. Shame was the most consistent thing in my life. It ruled me. Every thought about myself was rooted in shame, which then became the filter for all of my decisions. As I sat next to the upset 11-year-old me, I asked him how his heart felt. He replied, "Unseen, not valued, and not accepted." He didn't feel "good enough." The tough thing for me as a kid was that I felt exposed and disconnected, like I didn't belong. The big me approached the little me, sat down next to him, and began to talk to him about what he needed. I gave him the secret ingredient: compassion.

compassion [kəm'paSHən]

noun

sympathetic pity and concern for the sufferings or misfortunes of others: *the victims should be treated with compassion.*

- ORIGIN Middle English: via Old French from ecclesiastical Latin *compassio(n-)*, from *compati* '*suffer with.*'

I have a hard time admitting this, but I realized I had lived a majority of my adult life not knowing compassion. The best way to describe it was that I was hardened or calloused. The idea of being tender, soft, or nurturing wasn't even on my radar. I realized I spent a majority of life running without stopping. If I stopped, I expected something bad to happen. I would get caught, in trouble, or lose the life I had. Compassion came into my life when I stopped running and embraced the kid in me.

This child is alive in me as is the child within you. As soon as I began getting in touch with him, I started to see myself and my life differently. From nine years old until my forties, that kid ran. He didn't stop. He was scared, terrified, and running toward hope and away from people, places, and things that were a threat. The moment I started meeting with him and talking to him, he started to settle down and rest. I started making intentional time to ask him questions, discover his heart, and what was important to him. I also had to ask what he needed. No one had ever asked him that. When you start to show compassion to the child in your heart, you will find the keys to unlock your freedom, to remove your fears, and to give yourself permission to live in authenticity.

Our greatest weapon is compassion. What does compassion look like? Compassion is perfect love, and perfect love casts out fear. Where do we find this weapon? What is the source? This perfect love has only one source and is free and available to everyone. The love of God, our Creator, was exemplified by the sacrifice of His Son, Jesus: For God so *loved* the world that

He gave His only begotten son, that whoever should believe in Him would have everlasting life.

God, in His love for us, sent His Son to live and die for us that we might have freedom and access to the gift of eternal life, love, and hope. This is perfect love. This is amazing grace—a hope that cannot be stolen, that won't rot or fade. The life of Christ was Him living out the love of His Father, and by doing so, He showed us perfect love. This love from God is a gift of compassion when we didn't deserve it. It is incredible grace. The Bible states that even while we are sinners, Christ died for us (Romans 5:8). We don't deserve the love. We can't earn it, and we can't lose it; we only need to decide whether we want to accept it.

SELF-COMPASSION

Imagine this love is a gift in a wrapped box. This gift is what you are giving yourself—meaning that the adult you is going to be visiting the younger you at different times in your past, and you will deliver this gift and weapon to him or her. Love is compassion. Compassion is the key to unlocking the jail cell door and the shackles on your wrists. You're going to set yourself free with God's help.

This compassion was something I didn't possess for years. I had to learn and discover and accept it in my own heart. It played out especially in my parenting. I was frustrated that I wasn't like the other dads, being really caring and sensitive to the details of my kids' emotions. Once I received and embraced compassion for my heart, and the kid in me, immediately my heart and spirit took a drink off the fire hose of God's compassion and tender love for me. As a man who had a child within that was in a drought and desert of the soul, I needed this. This experience also transformed who I am as a father as well.

By the time I invited compassion in, my life was 80 percent what it could be. I was effective and productive in my marriage, parenting and career, but I felt like there was at least 20 percent of my mental hard drive that was corrupt. This corrupt memory was massively impairing my life. My self-talk and second-guessing became an inner dialogue that was driving me nuts. I actually thought I was going a little bit insane. The frustrating part for me was that I couldn't pinpoint what was wrong. In other words, I was experiencing the effects of the fear and shame, but couldn't see them clearly, let alone know how to locate and defeat them. I thought I was going to just have to suck it up and live life with this in the background.

As you have seen, this process requires going into some memories and past issues that you've locked away. Some people can get there quickly because they are willing to be vulnerable. Others will need a little more time to become vulnerable, but the desire to eliminate fear and find freedom will motivate you. In the greatest nightmares of our pasts lie the keys to experiencing God's love and glory. It is in the darkest moments of our lives that His light shines brightest.

This exercise and technique will require you to get quiet and have privacy. You will need your journal and the answers to the questions from the last chapter as well.

Any time you feel fear, shame, and especially negative self-talk getting the best of you, take about thirty minutes to an hour to get alone and process quietly. You're going to need to feel safe and secure in this place and time. Start with the feeling. Ask yourself whether you are feeling anger, sadness, loneliness, or fear. Fear is what we are after. When you think of fear, ask yourself, "In this situation, why am I not feeling good enough, valuable, seen, heard, or accepted?" Now take the feeling, such as not being accepted, and hold that emotion in the front of your mind. The next step is to travel back in time to the earliest memory of you as a child experiencing this emotion. Think hard. Most of the time I noticed that I had been playing these small memories in my head daily without realizing it, even though they were the echo of a trauma from years back. It could have been bullying at school; it could have been getting picked last on the playground, etc. The goal of the next step is to meet yourself as a kid in that exact memory. This can be scary and feel uncomfortable. It's a war with yourself, but it's so worth it.

I want to help you in this process as much as possible so that you can have the same weapon and strategy that I used. I will walk through an example of how I heal past trauma when shame rules me; this way you will know what to expect and learn how you can do this for yourself.

I first go into a session of prayer with the intent to heal. It's like mining for gold or coal. You go deep to discover. I focus on hunting down the fears and shame of the past that are currently holding me back and then wait to see what emotions rise to the surface. When I practice these sessions, I'm hunting. I am on a mission, and I'm planning on returning with something.

First, I believe that Jesus is the truth and He is love. He is safety and compassion. He contains everything you will need to make this journey and go through this exercise. No matter how scary, unsettled, or fearful you will feel, know that His perfect love casts out all fear (1 John 4:18).

During one of my healing prayer sessions, I saw a visual that I believe was given to me to help others. I imagined Jesus standing at the opening of a hole in the ground—a cave or a well. This cave dropped down about 100 feet. The well or cave is your past. You are at the base of the cave—the little you—the one from your past. Around Jesus' waist is a rope, which is glowing in righteousness, true love, and safety—the other end is tied to you. This is a bond of love that cannot be broken. In your possession, you have compassion and love in a gift box (your heart—where Christ lives) to be given to the younger you when you meet him or her.

For I am convinced that neither death, nor life, nor angels, nor principalities, nor things present, nor things to come, nor powers, nor height, nor depth, nor any other created thing, will be able to separate us from the love of God, which is in Christ Jesus our Lord.

PAUL THE APOSTLE (ROMANS 8:38-39)

Next, think of the current fear or shame that is overwhelming you. Take the fear and describe the feelings associated with it, which you are struggling against. Now, ask yourself when was the earliest memory you have when you felt these feelings. It could be as early as four or five years old. Think of this moment and this memory. Once you have accessed the memory, you need to see yourself. Hold that thought and imagine Christ lowering you into the pit. You are rooted in His love. Don't be scared to dive into the memory. Christ is in this with you and you are His son/daughter. You, as an adult, are tethered to Him and you cannot complete this process apart from Him. You are protected under His guidance in this process. There are hosts and legions of angels around you in protection as you make this journey and revisit this moment. I know it is intense but think of the freedom that waits for you on the other side.

You are now lowered to the bottom of the pit. During this time of prayer, I suggest focusing on one thing and one thing only—to have laser focus on you as a child. See yourself and think of those memories that stung or left an impression on you where you weren't heard or seen or valued. Think of what you were wearing, how you looked and every detail possible. I want you to focus on what I'm saying because this is very important. I want you to talk to yourself as a child—literally out loud. This act is you talking to your heart. Trust me, it can hear you. With eyes closed, talk to him or her and ask him or her how he or she are feeling in this moment. Focus on how he or she feels disconnected in the situation—unseen, unaccepted, not valued, or not heard.

When I got kicked out of the art contest, I was incredibly hurt. In this memory, as I sat next to 11-year-old me, I asked his heart how he felt. He replied, "Unseen, not valued, and not accepted." He described that he felt left out, cheated, and alone. As a kid, I often felt vulnerable and disconnected, as though I didn't belong. So the adult me approached the child me and offered him the secret ingredient: compassion. I approached him, sat down next to him, and began to talk to him about what he needed—compassion; though, to be honest, I didn't quite know what to tell the little me. I put my arm around him and said, "You are an incredible artist, and it was so amazing that they thought your dad did it. I am really proud of you and how well you did. Let's go out and celebrate."

Here's where it gets interesting. As I was in the bottom of the pit in the middle of this prayer doing business with my past, another memory hit me at that exact location. I saw my mother escorting me out of my third-grade class—I got in trouble for drawing in class, distracted from the teacher's lesson. My mother was furious. This incident was a very powerful event in my life, but I have always tried to stuff the memory away, discounting it as not a big deal. The crazy thing is that I was seeing two memories play out simultaneously. These two memories happened in the exact same hallway of my elementary school about thirty feet from each other. Crazy!

So while I watched myself on the bench and also saw myself getting escorted out, I addressed each one, walking up to each at the same time. I said to myself, "Buddy, I'm so sorry that this happened to you. I know this hurts. It really does. It stings and it's really frustrating. I'm so sorry. You are really an amazing artist and so gifted. You really make a lot of people happy with your gift. You got in trouble for drawing in class at an inappropriate time, I understand. You have a unique gift. Getting kicked out of the contest wasn't your fault. You did what you were supposed to do. I'm sorry they kicked you out. No matter what they think, Noah, you are an amazing artist. You have what it takes. No matter what they say, they can't take your gift and talent. It is part of who you are."

Now, for the first time, that child heard what he needed to hear. My body heard it. That child heard it from the true source—Jesus—the source who is saying these compassionate words through your heart. When people go through the process of healing themselves, I believe that it is ultimately Jesus who is doing the removal and disarming. We just have to be willing to take the journey into the pit and face the fears.

After compassion is offered, the child recognizes the truth of the event and can now let go. The memory still exists, but the trauma and power of it have vanished. It is cast out and replaced by love and compassion. Remember, our hearts as children long for connection. This connection is made by communicating acceptance and acknowledgment of the child's value. When compassion and love have been bestowed on our past self, the current self isn't triggered by the fear and shame that became false friends in the midst of these traumas. Even when these memories or challenges to my self-worth pop up now, I revert to my identity in Christ, take inventory, and see if I need to go down into the pit with the rope again.

As I came out of my prayer session, I began seeing myself differently. For the first time in my life, I truly understood God's love, and with it, a love of myself. It has also changed my perspective on my marriage and my kids.

THE "AFTERS"

So how will you know that your prayer healing session was effective? Well, there will be a feeling when you get to the other side of a healed moment that I call the "afters." I've discussed this with others who have experienced healing. Over the following days, weeks, and months, there are a few amazing things that take place. Here's what you can look out for:

The triggers or memories of the events no longer have power over you—

"For every child of God defeats this evil world, and we achieve this victory through our faith."
JOHN THE BELOVED (1 JOHN 5:4, NLT)

I remember being on the phone trying to put into words the feelings I was having. I don't know if I've ever experienced these feelings. They were one of an alignment with my heart, intellect, will, and body. For the first time, nothing was disjointed. I would even think back to the event or nightmare and all I saw or felt was love and compassion. My heart and my head knew it was true. I wasn't muscling my way through it or overcoming it by being positive. I am talking straight-up removal.

A peace that surpasses all understanding—

And the peace of God, which surpasses all understanding, will guard your hearts and your minds in Christ Jesus.
PAUL THE APOSTLE (PHILIPPIANS 4:7, ESV)

I remember walking around as if I had just gotten out of a war zone and was walking through a prairie or field—no noise and no racket. I felt completely safe and there was no second-guessing. I was experiencing a life with a spirit of permission, no longer constantly wondering if I was doing good or bad. I just felt settled in truth and authenticity.

Elimination of the feelings and zero symptoms—

*From his abundance we have all received one gracious
blessing after another.*

JOHN THE BELOVED (JOHN 1:16, NLT)

I waited to see if the feelings or thoughts would come back. I
even forced myself to face the events again. As I saw the event,
I didn't have any emotions except gratitude, compassion,
and love. Even some of the worst nightmares of my past
had become the greatest blessings, pointing me toward
compassion and love for my heart and for others.

An overwhelming amount of gratitude—

*Let the message of Christ dwell among you richly as you
teach and admonish one another with all wisdom through
psalms, hymns, and songs from the Spirit, singing to God
with gratitude in your hearts.*

COLOSSIANS 3:16 (NIV)

Life became less about dealing with the rock in my shoe or
about managing and dealing with pain. Life was freed up to
focus on gratitude and the hope that is everlasting and true.
Gratitude and thankfulness took my focus off of myself.

When you live in a world of uncertainty and dread,
consistency is an amazing comfort. School was one of the
few places I could find consistency and comfort. Even
though I hated school, I had stable, routine relationships and
mentorships with teachers that continued to grow—I could

only see these blessings that I had previously overlooked through this healing and the lens of gratitude.

Through gratitude, teachers became a nurturance and school met my need for mentorship. Through this new lens, I could see that my teachers were cool and a lot more of an influence than I thought. Looking back to grade school they were incredible influences on me and helped push me along toward my calling. I realize now how sensitive I was to everyone and everything around me, but I actually got along with the mean teachers that everyone else hated. I hated school but I loved learning drama, creative writing, art, and music. I had certain teachers stick around after school to help me craft entries for drum solo contests and help me start my art company from the rooms of my junior high art classrooms. These teachers were mentors in my youth who pointed me toward my strengths and my calling.

I now use the term "live upward and outward" as a motto in my daily life. Our basic desires default to self-gratification and being overly concerned with what we can get from life. Living upward and outward requires a daily discipline of turning our minds and wills over to God. "Be transformed by the renewing of your mind" (Romans 12:2). This truth is a great reminder that it doesn't just happen naturally. Turning away from our basic instincts requires us to intentionally live a daily life of renewing our thinking. As I said before, our choices and decisions are birthed from the mother ship of our brain. I treat my brain like a vehicle that needs an oil change every day for preventative maintenance.

Now it's time to do some serious work. Get out your ammo and lock and load.

#HUNTING TARGETS

1.   What is a childhood memory that still haunts you because of the shame or rejection that resulted from the event?

2.   Take this memory, go down into the well, and speak compassion to the child within you who has been hurt. Journal your experience. What do you see, say, hear, and feel?

3.   How does your heart feel now that you've walked the child within through this process? Are you experiencing any of the "afters"?

4.   Revisit this memory in a few days, weeks, or a month. Does the event still hold power over your life?

5.   Repeat this process as your self-talk leads you to other past traumas that have informed your identity.

PART THREE

WALKING OUT OF THE MENTAL PRISON: STEPPING INTO FREEDOM, AUTHORITY, AND LIVING IN YOUR CALLING

#CHAPTER 13

DISCOVER YOUR STRENGTHS

Strength does not come from winning. Your struggles develop your strengths. When you go through hardships and decide not to surrender, that is strength.[25]

ARNOLD SCHWARZENEGGER, ACTOR, GOVERNOR, TERMINATOR

Enter every activity without giving mental recognition to the possibility of defeat. Concentrate on your strengths, instead of your weaknesses … on your powers, instead of your problems.[26]

PAUL J. MEYER, ENTREPRENEUR, AUTHOR

AT THIS POINT IN THE BOOK, I HOPE THAT YOU HAVE taken the steps to become a fearhunter. I hope that you have shown compassion to those feelings of rejection in your childhood and experienced freedom from the power that these traumas once held over you. The remainder of the book is intended to help you to live an abundant, fruitful, and authentic life as a fearhunter now that your fears and shame are being attacked and eliminated. This book has hopefully helped you shift the way you think and approach your identity. This shift didn't come easily for me, and it didn't come right away; so press on and don't give up. It may take time.

One practice that has helped me make this identity shift has been to recognize and be true to the strengths and limitations that God has given me. Knowing your strengths and limitations is essential to live on the offense, not as a victim on the defense. I have even found that many individuals and companies that I consult suffer from not knowing their strengths, weaknesses, and unique value. Operating in your strengths leaves less room for fear and shame—which cause you to doubt yourself—and allows you to spend this precious energy on areas of great return.

The 2008 recession turned out to be an emotional season in our lives: Our son was diagnosed with autism, we lost my stepmom to cancer, and had to move due to financial strains. In the midst of this season, and perhaps because of it, I dove headfirst into my relationships with my mentors. I remember their kind and gentle patience with a guy like me, someone who wanted to get my calling written down on a piece of paper and walk out into the world to live it.

Alongside my mentors, I went through a journey of discovering my unique abilities, gifts, and passions and how

I could use them to positively impact my relationships with God, my wife, my children, and others. This breakthrough was achieved through an amazing exercise titled, "Now Discover Your Strengths" in a book called, *StrengthsFinder 2.0*. I am of the opinion that every human being would benefit greatly from reading this book. Discovering who you are supposed to be can be a lifetime of work. One of the best uses of your time would be to stop everything and take thirty minutes to measure yourself with the online Strengths Finder software test. The test results will give you the top five strengths you possess, giving you tremendous insight to how you are wired. These strengths became my filter of what I say yes to and what I don't. Using this filter, I began to trim anything out of my life that didn't play to one of my strengths. I stopped trying to fix who I wasn't and shifted that energy to playing to the strengths I do have.

I remember sitting with Steve, who came to me for some branding and consulting on his life portfolio. One of his biggest breakthroughs came when we defined his strengths rather than focusing on his weaknesses. Steve had worked for large brands that were major players in business. He had left the most recent company because he felt like he had reached his capacity for growth. He sat in my office, wondering about his next move, yet he hadn't taken stock of his strengths and what made him great. It's hard to sell yourself if you don't know what you are selling.

I encouraged Steve to take a moment to measure his strengths. Knowing where your strengths lie serves as a filter because it allows you the chance cut out the commitments that you have made that aren't in your wheelhouse. Fear makes its way into our lives when we start to second-guess and don't feel 100 percent confident in what we are offering the world. Fear and shame then get crafty in our heads. We feel like imposters, liars, posers, fearing that someone will find out that we really don't know what we are doing.

When I discovered my strengths, I was able to stop guessing and finally spend my time usefully. My greatest use of time, based on my strengths, includes: drawing or creating a painting, mentoring, brand architecture, consulting, and writing. Having confidence in these strengths allowed me to trim the fat and focus on my top strengths, which meant that I would have to stop spending my time on things that weren't of major value and impact.

As an example of eliminating my weak areas, I really dislike anything having to do with getting copies made, doing bookkeeping and reports; however, my publishing business in the art world requires that these things get taken care of. I did this work for years because it needed to be done and because I wanted to control every aspect of my business. I didn't trust anyone. I feared that no one could do it as well as I could, and I wanted and needed to know exactly everything that was going on. This controlling mindset is a way of thinking that will run you ragged. I realized it was the equivalent of a mechanic not only repairing the engine but also hand sewing the upholstery of the vehicles he worked on. Yes, I can do the bookkeeping, but it isn't my greatest use of time here. The moment I started to rid those unproductive things out of my life, fear and shame showed up like crazy.

People often get themselves into trouble by saying yes to everything that comes their way. Many do this to feed the ego of self-worth, or because they fear the conflict and potential rejection that would arise from saying no, and they also fear that the income they would pass up would be devastating and that they might lose out on future opportunities. They fear that the industry will pass them up. Saying yes to everything is a clear sign of not knowing your identity and your strengths. I was the king of yes. That's how I got myself into so much trouble with my time, my talent, and my money.

I remember when this idea hit home for me. I had spent the majority of the beginning of my career taking on any job I could find that would pay a dollar. I did everything from painting custom clothes at Nordstrom to doing tattoos on models for Motorola phone commercials. I was the guy that people would call for the most out-of-the-box jobs that no one else could do. There was one job in particular that will likely go down in my career as the most useless and time-consuming job. It was just before Easter and a friend of mine invented a large, ceramic dinosaur egg that was sealed and had candy inside. She needed three thousand of them painted in a short amount of time. I will never forget how upset I was at taking the job because there was nothing unique about the painting that was being done on them— anyone could paint the spots and "art" on them. Regardless of the income, it would have been wiser for me to broker the job and oversee the other artists, freeing me up to work on jobs that were unique to my skill set.

Life becomes extremely fun when you operate in the sweet spot of your calling and strengths. Now you might be saying, "Yes, but I need to make money, and I'm the one who has to get these jobs done." I understand; however, I am asking you to do two things: move forward each day staring fear and shame in the face, and eliminate the current daily activities and commitments that don't fit your strengths and sweet spot. As you move forward in each day, watch what you say yes to and don't be bullied by fear and shame. We don't need to allow shame and fear to bully us around each day forcing us to say yes to our false selves out of fear that others won't accept us or that they will walk away if we hold our ground in the truth of who we are.

Take a moment to discover your strengths and what makes you great. It's one of the most powerful tools to understanding what you have to offer. This filter is one of the greatest preventative measures to avoid signing yourself up for trouble. Fear and shame don't get an entrance into your life when you set healthy boundaries.

Filtering the choices and agreements that you make is powerful. You become super aware of the people you allow into your life. You filter every job that you say yes to. Your perception of time transforms as you realize that you don't want to spend a moment of your life on anything that doesn't matter. Live in what you are made to do, not just paid to do.

Boundaries are a great thing, especially when it comes to your identity. I spent the majority of my life reacting to everyone else's needs while forfeiting my own and wondered why I was so upset. I didn't know what I had to offer because I didn't know my strengths. It's hard to be effective when you don't know your assets.

Stop for a moment and measure your strengths. It can be a short exercise that will have immediate and powerful results. You will then have a filter, and this filter will help protect yourself from ... well ... yourself!

A Few Words About Work

We need to integrate our physical and spiritual realities in order to experience wholeness in our lives.

NOAH

I glorified you on earth, having accomplished the work that you gave me to do.

JESUS OF NAZARETH (JOHN 17:4, ESV)

I remember being a kid and staying at my grandparents' houses during the summers. I would often be woken up to my grandfather fixing breakfast and heading out the door at 4:30 a.m. It was like clockwork. One grandfather worked for Pacific Bell Phone Company for thirty-six years and the other worked for Quaker State Oil for thirty-six years. One worked without missing a single day in those thirty-six years. He was a great example of loyalty and integrity when it came to his work ethic.

Those memories have stuck with me and helped me navigate my work here on earth. I believe that a majority of us truly want to live in our calling, knowing that we are in God's will. We desire to live with purpose and passion. I understand the urgency to know your calling and the challenge to find it. One of the most important things I have learned is that your calling is likely what you already do in the workplace, and a shift in your perspective on work might reveal your powerful kingdom purpose as well.

I personally experienced this cognitive shift as I wrestled with how my career fit into the larger picture of calling and discovering God's will for my life. I came to faith when I was 9 years old and became a full-time creative at the age of 16, making art, signs, graphics, murals, and visual art for businesses and clients. As I grew up, I focused on doing all of those things more and better, becoming as successful in life as I could. I soon reached a ceiling of complexity when it came to my success; I had reached the top of what I could hope for my worldly career. My life was successful, but I didn't feel like it was significant. The moment I learned about significance and God wanting to use my life for His glory, everything changed. I asked myself, "Now what? What should I 'work' on? Do I continue doing art? If so, how do I use it?"

The New Testament shows us a great example of calling in a career through the apostle Paul. Before Paul was commissioned by God, he was highly educated and a high-ranking strategic religious leader. In line to be the next great rabbinical leader, Paul was charged with hunting down and destroying a new sect of Judaism called Christianity. Paul had talent and a passionate drive, but his life was pointed at the wrong target.

Paul was a tentmaker by trade. His career would take him around cities often requiring him to travel long distances. One day, the Lord interrupted one of his journeys on the road to Damascus. God temporarily blinded Paul to get his attention and show him the reality of His presence and existence. Once restored, Paul became passionate for the Lord, spreading the good news of who Jesus is and how people could come to know Him. Here is where it gets interesting: If I'm Paul, the moment I come to the reality of who Jesus is and the reality of the kingdom, I would want to abandon everything that doesn't align with this and make my full-time occupation being a traveling evangelist, right? Yet despite this radical conversion, Paul continued to make tents. What can we learn about our calling, purpose, talent, and career from his example?

Paul had some decisions to make as it pertained to his time, talent, and treasure. He had to figure out how he was going to stop putting points on the scoreboard of his life and start putting points on the scoreboard of heaven. He didn't abandon tent making to begin a full-time ministry; he used his genius and expert skills at tent making to fund his mission. More importantly, Paul leveraged his relationships and time during the week with his rope suppliers and fabric vendors to be used for the kingdom. He ministered to them and traveled as a tentmaker, preaching the gospel wherever he went. Paul wasn't working for the Lord just on weekends; he was on a mission all the time.

In my office, I help individuals strategically align their passions with their unique talents and capabilities. I mostly find that people hate their jobs and want to do more, feel more, and have purpose. It requires first understanding God's direction for their personal life and then discovering how God can use their abilities and talents for His kingdom like He did with Paul.

We all need to eat, put a roof over our heads, and support our lifestyles and families. Is it possible to live in the sweet spot of doing what you love most while making an impact and meeting your needs? You might continue working a normal job that may seem boring and lifeless, but with a new paradigm shift like Paul, you might come to see that God can use that boring career to support kingdom work on the side.

This career may be a steppingstone that allows you to fund new ventures and enhance ministries that the Lord presents as you step into living for Him.

Part of being a fearhunter is taking a daily inventory of these questions and areas of life to make sure that I'm stepping into the ideal life that God intended for me. Listen, we have to work. It's essential to our life and the Lord knows it. The question is, how will we leverage it? Will we coast as a ghost or be awakened and engaged for God's kingdom?

Paul leveraged his talent and skills to make money and further the kingdom. He took his entrepreneurship skills to help plant leaders and establish the first church. All Paul did was say yes to his assignment and stepped into risk and danger. He didn't have anyone providing him with a manual of "10 Steps to Evangelism and Church-Planting to Build God's kingdom." Paul stepped out in faith every day by waiting to see where God was at work and marching into the mix to help, using his vision, strategy, and talent. God took a guy who was good at tents and made him realize he was great at leveraging relationships, establishing a network, and getting people engaged.

So the next time you think your life is boring, and you don't have anything to contribute to the earth and God's kingdom, I would urge you to sit down and list what you are good at and where you come alive. Like Paul, you will probably see "making tents" as your career space, but your greatest contribution lies in your heart, in what you *know*. Ask God to illuminate and reveal the other dimensions of your soul and other talents that He can use to make an impact. Keep your job and make the people at your workplace your first mission field for the gospel. Then look around your community and life and find areas where you can add small doses of your passions or areas that make you come alive for God's kingdom. This could be serving, singing, meeting with others, helping build, helping plan, helping feed, teaching, anything you naturally enjoy that is beneficial to others.

Paul is one of the best fearhunters I've read about. He could have easily remained self-absorbed, pitying himself for his early life of being a Christian hater and killer. Instead, he overcame himself with God's help and focused every day on the reality of God's grace. Paul didn't have time for fear. He was focused on God's agenda of winning people's souls and depositing as much of God's currency into eternity as possible.

I meet many Christians who think that the point of life is only to fall in love with God and worship Him as much as possible. While this is healthy from a purely spiritual perspective, I believe it is critical to recognize that we follow and model our life after a Creator. He is in a constant state of newness and growth. Jesus rested while on His mission but He was "on mission" all the time. Work is a part of God's design. Jesus was here to do the will of the Father. As James, the brother of Jesus, rightly pointed out, the body without the spirit is dead, so faith without deeds is dead (see James 2). We need to integrate our physical and spiritual realities in order to experience wholeness in our lives.

We are called to live out our faith in all areas of life, and our work is no exception. Faith is a mental and spiritual position we hold, and the evidence that it has taken root in our lives is expressed through taking action. Living out our faith can be intimidating because it often involves risk and danger. Are you looking to get comfortable, or are you looking to grow and experience the fullness of who you are created to be? Is your life full of new risk? New work? New steps?

Our lifetime is one large action plan that stretches from beginning to end. The moment you internalize this idea, your perspective on growing older will change. Lost people live for the here and now and desire to gather enough riches to retire and grow old on a white sandy beach or golf course, yet lack an eternal focus or purpose. Their stories, experiences, and wisdom could be used to help others well into their golden years. I may someday reach an age where no one will hire me, but my life will be far from retired—retirement is not an option for me. I haven't found anywhere in God's Word talking about retirement. The last third of our life is when we will have accumulated the most wisdom and carry the most influence, knowing the most people we have ever known. This is prime impact time and is not the time to lay off the throttle.

Working on the kingdom while you are here on earth has major perks and is full of excitement. It's like gold digging. You work a vein of gold, which leads to other veins of gold that spring from it. As you carry out the current assignment, no matter how small, the Lord reveals new opportunities and expands the assignment. These new assignments include new relationships and opportunities for collaboration. However, this only happens in tandem with working out your faith and being in action mode. This way of life isn't rooted in duty or a forced obligation. We are compelled to live and act in faith as an act of worship and an offering of our love to God.

#HUNTING TARGETS

1. What strengths did you discover when you took the "Now Discover Your Strengths" assessment? What surprised you?

2. What strength have you been most neglecting to use for kingdom purposes?

3. Write out three ways that you can better draw boundaries on your time in light of knowing your strengths.

4. On a scale of 1-10, how would you rate your passion for your current career?

5. What would you need to make it a 10?

6. If you could design the ideal scenario of using your current job as leverage to underwrite your ministry or passion, what would you do? What are your ideas?

7. If you didn't have to make money from them, what are the dream jobs or assignments you've always wanted? Write out at least five ideas.

8. What is holding you back from building, launching, or investigating the possibilities of these assignments? Is it time? Structure? Other team members? Resources? Self-discipline?

#CHAPTER 14

THE DIFFERENCE BETWEEN A CALLING AND A CAREER

The chief condition on which, life, health, and vigor depend on, is action. It is by action that an organism develops its faculties, increases its energy, and attains the fulfillment of its destiny.[27]

COLIN POWELL, FORMER SECRETARY OF STATE, FOUR-STAR GENERAL

God did not direct His call to Isaiah—Isaiah overheard God saying, "… who will go for Us?" The call of God is not just for a select few but for everyone. Whether I hear God's call or not depends on the condition of my ears, and exactly what I hear depends upon my spiritual attitude.[28]

OSWALD CHAMBERS, EVANGELIST, TEACHER

One of the ways to identify your calling is to ask yourself if you would do the task for free.

NOAH

A S WE DISCUSSED IN THE LAST CHAPTER, CAREER IS often at the top of the list keeping us from the life we truly want to live. So many people are frustrated in their work. Their job isn't challenging, or maybe it's too challenging or isn't paying enough or leaves no room for advancement, etc. Just fill in the blank.

Career can be a touchy subject because it's often where many people find their identity. It is dangerous to have your identity be based on something you can lose or to allow someone else to provide your identity through your position at work. We need to separate our true identity as a dynamic and liberated child of God from what we do for work in order to really be free to dream about the ideal career path that suits our gifts and calling. There is a palpable irony in someone thinking about their dissatisfaction with their work daily, but they don't talk about it out of fear that they will lose their job, their security, or their identity. Without a job, many people are lost.

Here's what I think is fascinating: If you ask people if they like their job, they say yes. You then ask the same people if they feel that they are fulfilling their purpose in life, and they say no. Why do they stay in a job that isn't fulfilling their purpose? Often it is because they are paralyzed by fear of the unknown. It's my heart to help people get free from this trap. Ask yourself, what would happen if you tried to change jobs, career fields, or start your own venture?

I believe what is really bothering most people about their jobs is that it doesn't align with their calling. Our target is our calling. Think back to how Paul's perspective about tent making changed once he had a new purpose behind his traveling career. My mentor, Bob Shank, provided me with an easy way to differentiate between the two. He said, "Career is what you're paid to do; calling is what you're created to do." The reason why this is such a vital distinction is because it can help reveal to you where you are.

This example will help illustrate what I mean. Imagine walking into a mall. You might be hunting for a certain store or item. In order to find it, you first need to locate where you currently are. What is your current position? We look on the directory to find the "You Are Here" mark. Life is the same way. We can't find out where we are going unless we know where we currently are. Maybe you are saying, "lost," "alone," or "tired." You might say, "frustrated," "desiring more," or "sick and tired of being at the same location." Sound familiar? We often feel trapped by our career and don't know how or who can break us out of this prison. I am here to encourage you that you don't have to stay put. This book is about waking up the bear from hibernation.

This realization became clear to me in the early 2000s when I was building my company. My identity was found in success and achieving. Fear of failure and fear of letting people down was my measuring stick. I was run by fear; it got the best of me. Around age 28, I began to take inventory of myself through counseling and digging deep into my soul. I re-engaged with my mentors and started seeing my life through God's perspective rather than my own self-will. This process was a game changer for me.

At the time, career was being defined for me through society's lens: work as hard as possible; be a great provider for your family; and save all you can to retire and enjoy your later years. If you are lucky, you will leave your children a large inheritance. This message haunted me and constantly made me feel inadequate in my performance and achievements. I had to get to the bottom of the matter because my heart found no satisfaction in monetary success. I knew I had a gift of creativity, but I needed to find out what I was to do with it.

Being creative and doing art for major corporations and partnerships with companies like Disney and Universal Pictures were amazing achievements, but my heart longed for more significance rather than "success." This is where the identity crisis set in again. Career is what you are paid to do; calling is what you were created to do. Calling became my mission in life. I decided not to rest on what the world was offering me, but to investigate, search, and discover why God created me and put me here and then attempt to fulfill my assignment. Discovering your calling requires a guide, a mentor. I went through the process of discovering my calling and even partnered with my mentor to help people find theirs.

In the search for my calling as an adult, I learned that calling for me is to take the love of God and to minister that hope to as many people as possible. Most importantly, I needed to start with my family. My calling is to use the vehicle of creativity to reach as many people as possible to let them know that they are loved, that they matter, and that there is an amazing plan for their lives. There is a purpose, a hope, a joy that is everlasting that is not based on self-will. That is my calling. One of the ways to identify your calling is to ask yourself if you would do the task for free. It's the passion that charges the battery of your heart and doesn't drain it. After an eighteen-hour workday, you are ready for more because of your love for it and the impact you create with it.

Being a fearhunter means tracking down things that hinder my calling so I can eliminate them. I hunt the thoughts and beliefs that interrupt my communication with God and impair my calling. It is like pulling mental weeds on a daily basis. If we don't maintain the condition of our heart, it will default to agreeing with misbeliefs and lies. We must renew our minds in truth and remind ourselves of who we are and what the goal is. I am asking you to be intentional with your heart, loving yourself and giving yourself compassion. We have to renew our mind to stay rooted in truth. This maintenance is a discipline, a muscle to be trained.

In his book, *The War of Art*, Steven Pressfield talks about how much "resistance" will show up in your life as a result of moving closer to your calling and true self. This resistance happens because the true self wants to live in truth but is afraid of disconnection. The risk feels too great to live out our callings because it might mean the loss of approval, acceptance, favor, and love. This risk comes in many forms— friends, revenue, position, and influence. We believe the lie that all we have worked for will be lost if we come into the light of our true selves. What I have found is that the closer I move to my calling, the louder fear becomes. I fight against this fear by taking inventory of what's the worst-case scenario and finding the root of the shame keeping me from the goal.

When you sit down to do your inventory on your calling, it should be an accurate diagnostic on your heart and the condition of your soul because it should uncover the fears that are lurking within. Analyzing your life to discover your calling is a great way to measure how much of a grip fear and shame have on you.

#HUNTING TARGETS

1. If you were to say that you know your calling, what is it?

2. If you were to live as your true, authentic self, what would that look like?

3. If you lived out your calling and true self, where would you live? What would you be doing?

4. What are your biggest fears that come to mind when you think of letting everyone see the true you?

5. What might be the rewards or fruit of living out your calling?

6. What will the world gain from your true self and how will others benefit?

7. What actions, steps, or disciplines can you put into action tomorrow, this week, month, and year to move you toward living your calling?

#CHAPTER 15

BECOMING A PROFESSIONAL FAILURE

"What if I fall?" Oh, but my darling, "What if you fly?"[29]
ERIN HANSON, AUTHOR, POET

Failure is the key to success; each mistake teaches us something.[30]
MORIHEI UESHIBA, FOUNDER OF AIKIDO

WHEN I MET ONE OF MY FRIENDS, A HIGH-OCTANE LEADER, I noticed how the floorboards in his office weren't finished. As we talked, I heard about his business and portfolio of businesses. It sounded as if he was partly finished—in *everything* he did. I noticed that all areas of his life were on the edge of launch or on the edge of completion. It was a pattern. Because he feared the unknown, he was shaming himself into a false identity.

I spoke with him at length in his office over coffee. As we talked, he discovered the reality of what was going on. It was like a person emotionally vomiting the truth. He continued talking and eventually the truth rose to the surface and his soul spewed forth the reality. He said that he was afraid of exposure—of being seen. If he breaks through the surface and launches something, he will have to own the responsibility for his projects, and he might fail. He was always willing to dream big dreams and build them. The launching is what got him. It was like walking to the end of the diving board but being too afraid to jump. He was suited up, he was at the pool, he had climbed the ladder, but he stood paralyzed at the precipice.

The fear of the unknown can, at times, incapacitate us all. The price we pay for admission to an authentic, significant life is taking responsibility for the outcome when we move forward in the face of the unknown. We tell ourselves that if we launch or if we take the leap, terrible things will happen. We say we aren't good enough or don't deserve success. We say we won't know how to handle success or failure. We might lose a job, money, or connection from loved ones. We don't want to be cut off from love. But as we have discussed, our lives cannot launch if we are in a constant mode of fear.

I grew up seeing, hearing, and being told that creatives suffer. The "starving artist" was a mantra I regularly heard. It was like the world held creatives in a low-status position, expecting them to live on canned beans. However, it seemed that there were a few who branched out and escaped this self-fulfilling prophecy. But why so few? Out of the seven billion plus folks on this planet, why is it that only a few, and I mean a few, break out? Is fear a global epidemic? I think so. Fear is a part of our wiring as human beings. I believe that fear was designed by God for the healthy purpose of keeping us safe and wise, but often we use it to our detriment as a drug to medicate the actualized shame we might face if we fail. We need to learn to use fear to propel us forward out of awe and reverence; we need to learn to use fear as a fuel.

Taking the lead and being a trailblazer have prerequisites—you must be willing to become a professional failure, which requires being a fearhunter. You must be willing to own the responsibilities of the dream. Whether you are launching a new endeavor, a business, or a creative craft, there is a price to pay. It's the willingness to fall and fail and yet continue to get back up no matter what. Walt Disney leveraged everything in his financial life to build a crazy idea. Thomas Edison failed over eleven thousand times trying to invent the light bulb. Don't let failure slow you down.

SCARCITY VERSUS ABUNDANCE

Another prerequisite for taking a leadership role in your own life is believing that God has abundance in store for your life. This belief is strengthened when you are living in the sweet spot of His calling in your God-given identity. I remember as a teenager that things always felt tough in regard to our financial situation at home. Going out to eat was a big deal, and it felt like we were always chasing the dangling carrot of riches and wealth. At the time we were chasing wealth, we were also part of a great church in our city that was a part of our everyday lives. Oddly, it was seen as cool or trendy to be lowly in spirit within our church community—to be humble almost to the point of scarcity was noble. This scarcity thinking really messed with my mind.

I've spent the majority of my life thinking that life is supposed to be tough and that my life will be more significant if I struggle. I know, it's twisted. However, I came to realize much later in life that this way of thinking is extremely counterproductive to launching dreams and building amazing things. If I was going to be a part of helping build God's kingdom on earth as it is in heaven, it would require removing the ceilings of limitations, not just financially, but in every area of my life, including my time and my talent. As I write these words, I am preparing to meet a gentleman who wants to talk about taking my vision of mentoring, art gallery, and events together under one roof. It's likely the biggest dreaming I've ever done, but I keep coming back to the reality that if my dreams aren't intimidating to me, then they are most likely too small for God.

The ceiling of limitations on our lives is self-inflicted. Some of these false limitations are from our upbringing and our past, and they are our only frame of reference. As we leave home, we embark on the world with the goal of getting a safe career. We then waste our time trying to make life predictable and bring it under our control, even if it means forfeiting our dreams. If we aren't careful, we become a human existing rather than a human being.

Scarcity is another form of self-hate and an additional false mentality that we hold onto. We don't feel like we are good enough or that we deserve good things in our lives. We believe that living a life of faith means being lowly and downcast and that we must endure a lifetime of suffering (on occasion, our faith calls for a certain degree of suffering, but this is often the exception, not the rule). Many people see the faith in this light because believers act this way, and it doesn't look very attractive or fun. If I am a co-heir with Christ and I'm living out the calling of being an ambassador for my King, then I would hope that my attitude and posture are ones of attraction. Faith communities often try to push a productized set of beliefs rather than a promotional stance of invitation by example. The God I serve is in the business of doing things in excellence, so we should expect abundance, not scarcity. I've spent a great deal of my life making choices by avoiding what I wasn't supposed to do rather than focusing on all that I get to do because of who I am in Christ.

The moment I embraced the abundance mentality, my life became unstoppable. The key is that I wasn't driven by vain pride, but that I wanted to dream, build, and launch initiatives to help others and point people with God's love. It is difficult to build life-altering initiatives on a lowly spirit and a mentality of scarcity. Don't let this false belief, that life always has to be tough and that believers can't live a life of abundance and impact, be a limitation for you any longer!

You have to realize that you must go on the offense to eliminate these fears and remove your victim mentality. Living in scarcity will rob you of God's abundance and hinder the calling on your life. We must stop living on the defense; you don't score when you are on the defense. Life should not be lived only for ourselves but in service to Him and others. This is the best motivation for being on the offense there is-if we are liberated, we are able to liberate others and bring joy to God. The world is waiting for us to show up!

As you embrace your new life as a fearhunter, I would encourage you to keep the analogy of the arena or stadium on your mind daily. Visualize being the person who wants to be in the game. It takes knowing who you are. Are you a player or a backup? Have you seen yourself owning a uniform but never getting dirty, taking hits in the game? Do you know your position on the team/identity? Once you have your position, do you know your assignment? Now, are you willing to not only hit, but are you willing to take a hit? This is the price of admission—to be willing to take a hit. My goal is to help you understand that it isn't just playing for the sake of risking and failing. It's gaining the clarity of knowing what team you're playing for, what the reward is, and what your specific role is on the team. And remember, the one who scores the most points is the one who has possession of the ball most of the game, living on the offense, not the defense. It's those who know their position (identity), know their assignment (calling), and who they are playing for who lean into risk and win the prize.

Living a life of authenticity will require you to take what you have learned thus far and put it into practice. You must continually develop your relationship with God so that you have the correct perspective and unity with kingdom ideals. You have to turn away from shame and fear by hunting down the past traumas that have implanted lies into your mind. You must know your strengths to begin to know your true identity and to find the calling that God is leading you to. You must believe that God wants abundance for your life. Lastly, you must be willing to fail in all of this. You might fail as you move toward something that you believe God is calling you to, but even in this failure, you will get closer to living your authentic life.

Get in the game; take the hits; fail and score. It's better than sitting on the sidelines or in the stands. Make failure your new business, and you truly will be a fearhunter.

#HUNTING TARGETS

1. What dreams have you put aside for fear of having to take responsibility for their success or failure?

2. In what areas of your life do you need to become a professional failure to move forward in faith toward accomplishing your dreams and goals?

3. Do you see your life in abundance, or are you always taking a minimal approach to your time, talent, and money?

4. Are you using scarcity in your thoughts about your self-worth, thinking you are never good enough?

5. Do you keep creating ceilings of limitations on your finances out of fear of success?

6. If you wrote down what it looks like to make your decisions based on abundance, what decisions might you make today in the way you see yourself, your time, and money?

7. What fears and lies do you continue to agree with that keep you in scarcity?

8. What dreams have you put on hold due to the ceiling of your beliefs and limitations? Do you agree that these are self-inflicted?

#CHAPTER 16

AIMING FOR SIGNIFICANCE

In the end, our life won't be measured against others. We will be measured against the potential we had and the influence we had on others.

BOB SHANK

It's not an accident that musicians become musicians and engineers become engineers: it's what they're born to do. If you can tune into your purpose and really align with it, setting goals so that your vision is an expression of that purpose, then life flows much more easily.[31]

JACK CANFIELD, MOTIVATIONAL SPEAKER, AUTHOR

What would you do with yourself and your life if money was removed from the equation?

NOAH

HAVE WE COME TO ACCEPT A LIFE OF JUST GETTING BY? Have we settled for living paycheck to paycheck and measuring our happiness and success by our ability to get the bills paid? This standard of living fascinates me because I've noticed that even when the bills get paid, we still aren't happy. Most folks who win the lottery end up worse than they were before they won. Our entire security, purpose, and value have been determined by the amount of money we have in our bank accounts. Amassing wealth and chasing our culture's carrot that having enough will bring the happiness that is "just beyond the horizon" is a lie. That kind of happiness is contingent on circumstances. Joy, however, is everlasting and is based on your true identity in knowing God and in knowing who He created you to be and do regardless of money.

Most people believe that the fears and issues they battle can be solved with money, and the more money they have, the less fear will be present in their lives. This begs the question—why, when people have so much money, can't they get rid of the fears? Why do so many folks end up in rehab and sometimes even numb themselves to death when they become wealthy?

I came to the conclusion that neither several months' reserve in the bank nor twelve years' reserve in the bank would change my outlook on myself or the condition of my happiness. This takes me back to the heart of the matter: passion. What would you do with yourself and your life if money was removed from the equation? It's a great exercise to maintain as an inventory for your life. The amount of money people have often keeps them from taking action on following their passion and building their dreams. When helping with brand strategy for companies, I have noticed that most people feel that their passions and dreams are an afterthought. They won't overcome the fear of risk until the risk is minimized by having enough money to act as a buffer. To them, cash equals security, so as soon as they have enough to feel secure, they will then begin to build their dreams. I believe that the answer to living authentically, following our passions, and building our dreams boils down to our main driving force in life: what is our purpose?

A recent conversation at an art show in San Francisco illustrates this point well. I struck up a conversation with a kid behind the counter of a nearby store. He was a pleasant young man, so I felt comfortable asking him some fun experimental questions. I asked him about his passions; what is the thing in life that truly fires him up? He said that it was making people happy and seeing them smile. Immediately I thought, *That's cool. I wonder how he could build a life and make a living from that?* Maybe he should work at Disneyland? Just kidding. But it would be a good start. I then asked, "If I put one hundred million dollars into your bank account and you traveled and got everything out of your system, how would you spend the rest of your life?" He was a little shy, but then he said, "I think I would just hang out with my dog. My dog means a lot to me." I then asked him, "What about twenty years from now?" He said he didn't know. This kid seemed to suffer from a lack of purpose.

I don't believe that this lack of purpose is isolated to young people. I often have the privilege to speak around the country, and one of my favorite things to discuss is the process of moving from success to significance. Throughout the talk, I show slides of what success looks like to the general culture. The images consist of supercars in front of mansions, white sandy beaches, and bungalows over a crystal clear ocean. It seems to me that everyone is wearing themselves out trying to create a piece of heaven on earth. I then share images that portray what most people don't realize is true: most often, these extravagant and luxurious people are bored. They take these fabulous vacations and buy extravagant things to distract themselves from their empty lives. Most people desire to get to that place and live that lifestyle but then experience emptiness once they get there because they aren't living for significance, but for worldly success. I've also found that many even fear success because they will no longer have a purpose to live for once they've achieved success.

Without purpose, we have no direction. We are all on different journeys, but we are going to end up at the same destination and will be asked the same questions. The weight of eternity should affect our immediate actions today. Thinking this way is a freight train of a paradigm shift. If you internalize and act on it, you will go from wavering in your purpose to a conviction in your purpose, desiring to live in such a way that everything you do brings glory and honor to God.

> *Whatever you do, work at it with all your heart, as working for the Lord, not for human masters, since you know that you will receive an inheritance from the Lord as a reward. It is the Lord Christ you are serving.*
>
> COLOSSIANS 3:23–24 (NIV)

Finding our purpose leads to living a life of meaning, true connection, and fulfillment. It's easy to default to finding purpose in our career because it means we do something, get money, and put food in our mouths. This purpose meets the basic needs of survival; however, if our heart and calling are not in it, we quickly lack enthusiasm and resentments set in. Your soul knows when it's not getting fired up, when it is wasting time, and not operating in its natural talents.

KINGDOM STEWARDSHIP

The gospel says that our citizenship in the kingdom has been gifted to us, made possible by the works of God on our behalf as a result of the sacrifice of the Lamb of God on the cross. No one can earn this gift; the works of humans cannot satisfy the expectations of our Holy God to gain entrance into His domain—this is a relief on our part because our acceptance into His kingdom and receiving His unconditional love are not based on our achievements, but upon the favor and blessing that He enjoys lavishing upon us.

Once redeemed, we are infused with a kingdom purpose, and our life becomes focused on bringing the reality of God's kingdom to be experienced on earth. Jesus taught us this when He showed His disciples to pray for His Father's will to be done "on earth as it is in heaven" (Matthew 6:10). As kingdom residents, God has freely given us gifts and opportunities to help build this kingdom, and we then become stewards of all He has given us. He has heavily invested in our lives because He knows our *true* value and that we are capable of achieving great things. God welcomes us just as we are but always sees the potential outcome of who we *can* be, rather than seeing the shortcomings of our current situation.

Consider a parable of Jesus that demonstrates kingdom stewardship:

After a long absence, the master of those three servants came back and settled up with them. The one given five thousand dollars showed him how he had doubled his investment. His master commended him: "Good work! You did your job well. From now on be my partner."

The servant with the two thousand showed how he also had doubled his master's investment. His master commended him: "Good work! You did your job well. From now on be my partner."

The servant given one thousand said, "Master, I know you have high standards and hate careless ways, that you demand the best and make no allowances for error. I was afraid I might disappoint you, so I found a good hiding place and secured your money. Here it is, safe and sound down to the last cent."

The master was furious. "That's a terrible way to live! It's criminal to live cautiously like that! If you knew I was after the best, why did you do less than the least? The least you could have done would have been to invest the sum with the bankers, where at least I would have gotten a little interest."

JESUS OF NAZARETH (MATTHEW 25:19-27, THE MESSAGE)

God desires to bless us with rewards based on the heavenly outcome of our efforts, and ultimately, our treasure in the kingdom is based on the results of our stewardship on His behalf. The Scriptures tell us that these efforts will be evaluated at the judgment seat of Christ. Pleasing God in this lifetime—by aligning with His plans for us, in His kingdom—is the goal, and God's recognition and rewards are offered as our incentive. It is crucial to understand that this is a reward system and not a system of gaining acceptance or love from God.

The gospel celebrates the works of God, performed for *us,* while our stewardship of His kingdom celebrates the works of the redeemed, performed for *God.* These principles work hand in hand to accomplish the work of God in our world. This principle of kingdom stewardship is very important to understand—this is our purpose as ambassadors of His good kingdom.

FOUR KINGDOM PRINCIPLES

For the redeemed, kingdom stewardship offers clarity that is precise and powerful. Consider four kingdom principles:

1. God loves you and has a wonderful plan for your life, both now and throughout eternity.

2. You are now in Christ and are called to participate in His plan, which is called the Great Commission.

3. His plan for you, within His greater plan, is for you to fulfill the unique destiny for which He made you. This is your kingdom calling.

4. Your work in fulfilling His plan will please Him and you will produce an eternal value, for which you'll be recognized and rewarded.

PLEASING GOD

Receiving God's kingdom invitation through the gospel is the beginning of a journey that marks the transition from spiritual death to eternal life. If the Christian life is a journey, what is the destination at the end of the road?

> *So we make it our goal to please him, whether we are at home in the body or away from it. For we must all appear before the judgment seat of Christ, so that each of us may receive what is due us for the things done while in the body, whether good or bad. Since, then, we know what it is to fear the Lord, we try to persuade others.*

PAUL THE APOSTLE (2 CORINTHIANS 5:9–11, NIV)

Pleasing God *is* the journey, and the judgment seat of Christ is the checkpoint at the end of life to measure our success in that endeavor, that He may reward us accordingly. That has always been the objective; it's kingdom stewardship in action.

> *Now faith is confidence in what we hope for and assurance about what we do not see … and without faith, it is impossible to please God because anyone who comes to Him must believe that He exists and that He rewards those who earnestly seek Him … All these people were still living by faith when they died. They did not receive the things promised; they only saw them and welcomed them from a distance, admitting that they were foreigners and strangers on earth … Instead, they were longing for a better country—a heavenly one.*

SUMMARY OF HEBREWS 1

Pleasing God is a lifelong objective for those living in faith. This passage, citing the great names of Old Testament history who had pleased God, recognizes two necessary factors in the lives of those who accomplished that objective:

1. They believed that God exists; that belief was based on His self-revelation, not their own constructed theologies and religious assumptions.

2. They believed that chasing after His promises—"rewards"—was worth devoting their lifetimes to doing.

This was not a multiple-choice exercise; the writer of Hebrews found both ingredients present in the motivational mix of those who lived out a robust faith in God.

FROM GOOD TO GREAT

As we place our faith in Jesus, we are made righteous; this is the gift that keeps on giving.

God's goodness has been imputed to His family. If goodness is now our baseline, is greatness a conceivable pursuit?

> *Therefore anyone who sets aside one of the least of these commands and teaches others accordingly will be called least in the kingdom of heaven, but whoever practices and teaches these commands will be called great in the kingdom of heaven.*

JESUS OF NAZARETH (MATTHEW 5:19, NIV)

Jesus called them together and said, "You know that the rulers of the Gentiles lord it over them, and their high officials exercise authority over them. Not so with you. Instead, whoever wants to become great among you must be your servant, and whoever wants to be first must be your slave—just as the Son of Man did not come to be served, but to serve, and to give his life as a ransom for many."

JESUS OF NAZARETH (MATTHEW 20:25-28, NIV)

We are promised a place that is beyond imagination and requires a revelation from God to even begin describing its wonders. This is the universal promise to all who believe and are now defined by the goodness they've received from God. This is the promise of the gospel. The invitation to *greatness* is the compelling benefit offered as a result of our role in kingdom stewardship. Those who choose the extraordinary pursuit of life on earth in service to the purposes of God and the directions of His kingdom will achieve greatness in the kingdom and will be promoted into a level of eternal experience that is stored up for us as treasure by our atypical commitment in this life.

GOSPEL OPPOSITION

You have to expect spiritual warfare whenever you stand up for righteousness or call attention to basic values. It's just a matter of light battling the darkness. But the light wins every time. You can't throw enough darkness on light to put it out.[32]

THOMAS KINKADE, ARTIST

The enemy of God has worked since the creation of man to thwart God's purposes in His creation. From the fall in the garden until now, God's truth has been subverted by Satan's counterfeits. God is the source of all that is good, and the evil one poisons and perverts the good at every turn. Paul tells us to "not be ignorant of his (the devil's) devices," and also to "put on the whole armor of God that you may be able to stand against the schemes of the devil"; therefore, we need to be aware of common lies that keep us from pursuing the truth.

The gospel is corrupted when the evil one proposes good works as the means to gain redemption. Cults have always been founded on salvation strategies that emphasize good works as a method of earning God's favor rather than by our receiving salvation by God freely pouring His good favor upon us. The principles of kingdom stewardship are corrupted when the evil one proposes that because good works are not the means for salvation, then neither are they valuable in gaining greatness in heaven along with eternal rewards. Fruitless faith is founded on an embrace of God's grace for salvation but then rejecting our calling of walking in good works done in faith to bring Him joy.

THE SHREDDER OR THE VAULT

A lot of folks set themselves up for failure by believing lies that the world advertises to them. Our fear-based culture tells us, "If you don't have a particular lifestyle, you will not be valuable in the eyes of society and neither will you be fulfilled." I took this bait while I was first growing my business. I believed that I needed to make as much money as possible to make my wife happy and to provide for my kids.

I felt pressure to diversify my wealth in real estate and grow my investments. I ended up wearing myself out physically, spiritually, and mentally by trying to meet these pressures, and I became a toxic mess. I had no time and was constantly angry and frustrated because I wasn't meeting culture's measuring stick that defined success. I had created, without knowing it, a chrome-plated hamster wheel that I would jump on every day and run at 150 miles per hour. I was so intoxicated by success and finding security that I burned out. I became really upset with myself because I had been chasing after a fantasy. Most successful folks on jets and driving fancy cars will tell you that they are living the dream. But it's only "the dream" so long as it's for the right purpose, and more importantly, for the right *Person*.

For what will it profit a man if he gains the whole world and forfeits his soul?

JESUS OF NAZARETH (MATTHEW 16:26, ESV)

The turning point for me was in realizing that the fears, shame, resistance, and demons could not be eliminated or solved with money. These are soul issues. Purpose and true meaning are right under our noses waiting to be taken. The image of eternity changed everything for me, for my purpose, for my mission, and for dealing with fear and shame. Why? Because when you know you have limited time, you start making drastic decisions and moving straight toward a life of producing fruit—fruit that lasts. So what does this look like?

In regard to my time, talent, and treasure I have two choices: either deposit them in a shredder or in a fireproof vault. In the end, our life will be measured, and will we stand before our Creator. He will ask us, "What did you do with what I put in front of you, My child?" In other words, how did you leverage your time, talent, and treasure to invest in things that will last forever, on into eternity?

> *By the grace God has given me, I laid a foundation as a wise builder, and someone else is building on it. But each one should build with care. For no one can lay any foundation other than the one already laid, which is Jesus Christ. If anyone builds on this foundation using gold, silver, costly stones, wood, hay or straw, their work will be shown for what it is, because the Day will bring it to light. It will be revealed with fire, and the fire will test the quality of each person's work. If what has been built survives, the builder will receive a reward. If it is burned up, the builder will suffer loss but yet will be saved—even though only as one escaping through the flames.*

PAUL THE APOSTLE (1 CORINTHIANS 3:10–15, NIV)

Let's remember what God ultimately values. He gave His one and only Son for humanity, thereby demonstrating that people and relationships are His ultimate value. This means that our success should also be based on an entirely different measuring stick than what we often prioritize. My life went from success to significance the moment I got on God's agenda in understanding what true purpose and significance are. This idea provides motivation for what we do today, this week, this month, and for a lifetime. A life that seeks significance is one that builds community and shows love for both the church *and* those outside the church. Building and highly esteeming healthy relationships brings glory and honor to Jesus—the author of relationship. Where are you investing your time, talent, and treasure?

FEARLESS IN THE GIVING OF YOUR TREASURE

The idea of the shredder and the vault really hit home for me when it came to our money. Whenever I speak with individuals on their personal brand, I regularly hear the same end goal: "I want to provide for my family, and then once I have that taken care of, I want to give to the needy and help others." I totally understand this thinking. The world does a fantastic job at keeping us distracted from giving with the "provide for your family" mentality. My life was turned upside down in a great way when the idea of stewardship took root in Chantel and my giving. I spent years stewarding my time and my talent, but giving and money was always something I saw doing in the future. If I had to do it over again, I would begin as a professional giver. I am now working with my children to help them begin their lives this way.

With these new revelations, I was compelled to get my life in order regarding how I stewarded *all* of my resources. This included how I spent my time, figuring out how to best steward my gift of creativity and also my revenue and success. Things had to move toward significance, not only success. This area of giving is where fear hunting made a massive impact on my life. I grew up in a family where money was scarce, and therefore everything else was also viewed as a scarcity: time, talent, and treasure. The truth was that talent existed in abundance, but we were scattered in mission, focus, and giving. I remember that my grandparents were consistent in charity and their giving; however, it didn't take root in my life for quite some time. I gave out of guilt rather than from a position of joy.

As I got older, the idea of stewardship went into hyperdrive when I embarked on my mentorship with Bob Shank and his system of intentional mentoring and coaching called "The Master's Program." Over various course sessions and coffee time together, we worked toward restructuring my time, talent, and treasure to get into the sweet spot of stewardship for a life of significance, not just success. Little did I realize that this program would actually have me on a journey of earnest fear hunting.

When we think about the question that we will be asked at the end of our lives, it pulls things into focus quickly. The most motivating factor for taking action is time. If I know that the hand is ticking on my kingdom clock, then it allows for my decisions to be hyper focused on what I do, how I do it, and most importantly, why I do it.

WHO HOLDS THE MEASURING STICK?

In the end, our life won't be measured against others. We will be measured against the potential we had and the influence we had on others.

BOB SHANK

I spent my 20s climbing the ladders of success, realizing they were all leaned up against the wrong buildings. I defined who I was by what others thought of me and by how well I performed. The measuring stick of my worth was in the wrong hands. After doing serious work on our hearts through

God's grace, we see that the measuring stick is now out of the world's hands, and our worth is measured by an entirely different set of standards. My self-worth isn't based on my net worth. We often project society's thoughts onto ourselves, fear letting other people down, and put the measuring stick back into others' hands. I want to encourage you to focus on your heart. The new you, according to how your Creator sees you, is in contrast to how the culture sees your worth, and His approval is what's most important.

> *Therefore if anyone is in Christ, he is a new creature; the old things passed away; behold, new things have come.*
>
> PAUL THE APOSTLE (2 CORINTHIANS 5:17)

There are two standards by which I measure my life. I first remind myself, as a standard, that I am no longer bound to performance. My identity in God says, "I am who I am regardless of what I *do*." The second standard by which I measure myself is by asking whether I'm using my time, talent, and treasure for kingdom purposes, believing that I will see rewards in eternity as a result of my stewardship. Kingdom purpose means that my life isn't only about me; I want to help others, not for approval or worth, but to express the love that I've been shown.

I've spent a majority of my life trying to fix myself while having little impact on the lives of others because I was too busy focusing on myself. Here's the secret: you get fixed when God takes over and you live your life out of gratitude, which also enables you to positively impact others. You get fixed in the process of helping. As you discover the heart of God, you, in turn, realize how much you are loved, cherished, and adored. You can't expect to give compassion to the world and others if you haven't first received it yourself. You cannot give what you do not have.

> *For we are his workmanship, created in Christ Jesus for good works, which God prepared beforehand, that we should walk in them.*
>
> PAUL THE APOSTLE (EPHESIANS 2:10, ESV)

Being a fearhunter comes with the responsibility of removing the beliefs and other hindrances that impair our effectiveness. I believe that at the end of my life, I won't be compared to others and how well they did, nor will I be judged by how much money I made while on earth—that's not God's measuring stick. God will bring into account all the resources and potential that I had to make a positive influence for His kingdom. It's up to me, as an ambassador of His love, to get my life in order to effectively steward my time, talent, and treasure. We can live on the offense (hunting), or we can be a target of this fallen world and live in its fear. We are not here to barely manage—we are here to thrive.

> *I came that they may have life and have it abundantly.*
>
> JESUS OF NAZARETH (JOHN 10:10, ESV)

#HUNTING TARGETS

1. Where have you received your outlook on giving?

2. How does life look now knowing that you don't have to settle for good when God invites you into greatness?

3. Knowing that you don't have to live in scarcity, how does this chapter reveal God's heart toward you and your life?

4. Since loving God, loving people, and making disciples is our calling, how could those be implemented in your daily and weekly life?

5. What decisions or choices in life are you afraid of living out because you fear being exposed?

#CHAPTER 17

DECISIVE VICTORY: YOUR TRUE AUTHENTIC SELF

We need to find the courage to say no to the things and people that are not serving us if we want to rediscover ourselves and live our lives with authenticity.[33]

BARBARA DE ANGELIS, PH.D., RELATIONSHIP CONSULTANT, TV PERSONALITY

Authenticity is the alignment of head, mouth, heart, and feet—thinking, saying, feeling, and doing the same thing—consistently. This builds trust, and followers love leaders they can trust.[34]

LANCE SECRETAN, LEADERSHIP THEORIST

AS A BOY, THERE WAS A CRUCIAL PERIOD OF TIME WHERE I was bullied and harassed. I remember this physical education class that I took in the eighth grade vividly. After class was over, all of us boys smelled to high heaven yet still had the rest of the day to spend at school. For some reason I was the only boy who would shower; I couldn't stand the idea of body odor and sweat for the rest of the day. I remember being really embarrassed and concerned about my body. The boys made fun of me for being the only one naked out of the thirty other guys. We lived in an area where it could get down to thirty degrees in the morning. I would strip down, keep my back to the crowd, and freeze. I remember the fear each day as PE would finish. However, the feeling of a strong workout and sweat followed by a clean crisp shower was so refreshing, it was all worth it.

I think the showers played a key role in my identity growing up. I might not have the shape and body I wished I had, but I was being myself. By taking showers, I kind of set the tone for the other guys. Soon, a couple of other guys started to take them and there were a few by the end of the year. I had to care more about what mattered to me rather than make my decisions based on what I thought the others would feel or think. I remember being called names and having them make fun of my body. This was a moment of authenticity for me growing up, but these were few and far between.

Now, thinking about my own kids having to take showers in front of their whole class almost brings me to tears. It's the act of facing fear and shame with the courage to be yourself that really moves me. I wouldn't want them being exposed to the possibility of, let alone endure, being taunted by their peers.

I share this story because it perfectly illustrates the fact that living our authentic lives often means that we must drop the proverbial fig leaf. Even though I was made fun of for showering, it proved to me that our true identity requires exposure and the risk of being seen for who we truly are. Full exposure before God and man means we have to let down our guard and our carefully crafted external façade. Fear hunting mandates hunting down the fears and shame that we have allowed to rule us, embrace the reality of them, eliminate them, and then drop the leaf. It takes a lot to keep the leaf in place—running life with one hand holding the leaf and doing the rest of life with the other hand is difficult to manage!

I had to ask myself what might happen if I lived authentically, being true to who God created me to be. I imagined embarrassment and failure as well as not being accepted and experiencing loss of connection. Alternatively, in the name of self-preservation, I would play life safe, stonewall my feelings, and hide my identity to live a lie.

I want to encourage you to be proactive to monitor your heart and daily drop the fig leaf. Be intentional in the ongoing maintenance of your true identity by using the chapters in this book and the hunting targets to proactively fight fear and eliminate it. Don't allow fear to trick you; we can erase the fear and shame of the past that have held us back, but as we move forward into new seasons in life, we can make new agreements with subtle lies without recognizing it. I have found I have to stay in an inventory mode on my heart weekly and sometimes even daily because there is an enemy who doesn't sleep. He works 24/7 and changes his strategy to try to take me down. He doesn't want me to be effective, to see my dreams getting launched, and he certainly doesn't want people coming to know God's love. The more my faith increases and my life progresses God's mission, the enemy will run greater interference. It's expected because that's the war we fight, and it's actually the fight that continually makes us stronger.

Dropping the fig leaf requires vulnerability, and it requires courage, but the payoff has such great rewards. God has designed you and me as one-of-a-kind originals, and His craftsmanship isn't flawed. He creates masterpieces. We are fearfully and wonderfully made.

> *I will give thanks to You, for I am fearfully and wonderfully made; wonderful are Your works, and my soul knows it very well.*
>
> KING DAVID (PSALM 139:14)

#HUNTING TARGETS

1. Daily ask yourself, "If I could be and do anything I wanted in glorifying God with my time, talent, and treasure, what would I do today?"

#CHAPTER 18

PREVENTATIVE MAINTENANCE FOR ACTIVE DUTY

The keys to brand success are self-definition, transparency, authenticity and accountability.[35]

SIMON MAINWARING, BRAND CONSULTANT

If we eliminate the distractions, we will have a new capacity for great things to come into our lives.

NOAH

REMEMBER, THE REASON WE WANT TO BECOME A FEAR-hunter is to eliminate the fear, guilt, and shame that stand between us and the life we were created to live. As we grow in wisdom, it will require that we perform a little housecleaning in order to be free. More importantly, if we eliminate the distractions, we will have a new capacity for great things to come into our lives. The goal is to spend our lives working on only great projects—being a self-disciplined steward of our time, talent, and treasure—that will have an eternal impact. We want to graduate from a life of management to a life of abundance and freedom in our calling. We want to move from success to significance.

You may be mad as you think of the time you've wasted not living your true self, but let's not fall back into shame. Lighten up on yourself; there's nothing to do but look forward. Just be glad you are finally starting to put this behind you now and not later. These remaining pages are the disciplines to daily focus on the truth in your thinking, so let go of being mad at yourself. Embrace the truth of who you are and where you are headed. Repeat these steps daily and hourly as you reformat your brain. It is then that you will be living with confidence in how God designed you, living out a life of worship to Him without fear.

Below are a few questions to consider prayerfully that I personally still use to take inventory in my life and do a spiritual oil change on my soul daily, weekly, and monthly. The past chapters have been about elimination. As you begin to remove the fear and shame from your life, let's discover the true you—not the fake you that you've worked so hard to maintain. Ask God to reveal the lies hidden deep in your heart:

1. Where have I been hiding?

2. What do I not want people to find out about me?

3. What are the lies that I keep agreeing with that I use to define myself?

4. What are my habits and behaviors that I don't like about myself?

5. What areas in my life are destructive that I do out of self-medicating to run from shame or guilt?

6. To whom can I talk and disclose these answers to release myself from my false self?

7. What mental agreements do I make that create ways to hide out, numb myself, or escape?

ACTION STEP: DO SOME SOUL SEARCHING.

The True Identity: Your Unique Superhero Weapon-We are on earth for a purpose. We have been given a secure, unique identity in God's overall plan while we are here. It is our job to discover and capitalize on this unique calling. We don't have much time. After being on this earth for forty-four years, I can tell you that the vast majority of people I have met believe that life is about growing up, making money, and grabbing all you can before death. I have seen countless individuals frustrated in youth, burnt out in midlife, and cranky in old age because life had flat-lined without purpose. I've learned that we are wired and designed to not only discover the love of God and our identity but also to discover how to best live it out. It is a result of His "love in action" through which we find our purpose and reason for existing.

As I've read God's Word, His agenda is action—faith in action. I'm convinced that our lives are an act of worship in how we use our time, talent, and treasure as a praise to Him. This is the true north on your compass of following Him in your hunt. When life gets you down and you feel lost, remember the truth of your identity and mission. Your agenda is His agenda. This is the heart of what defines our purpose. This truth brings so much clarity to life and eliminates the need to manage our false selves. I couldn't think of anything more exciting than discovering our talents and unique identities to live out, helping others, and glorifying our Creator while in the process. Our lives are solutions for others' problems. If you are willing to discover your unique superhero power, your life will come into focus and your mission will become clear.

I believe that all humans have a craving to know our true selves and to belong to a right and good mission in life. True identity is found in God because we were created in His image with a destiny to be like Him. I seriously felt like I had won the lottery when I found this treasure of truth through my mentor. It was exactly as God's Word reveals: "The kingdom of Heaven is like a treasure that a man discovered hidden in a field. In his excitement, he hid it again and sold everything he owned to get enough money to buy the field" (see Matthew 13:44).

Your identity is the foundation of your life, and it's the most important work you will ever do for yourself. I teach and mentor individuals through my office, and the main goal of everyone I meet is that they want to build an amazing brand and audience. Very few are even aware of the importance of the foundation of identity. When I consult brands, it becomes evident quickly if the company wants to build a brand for success versus significance. They get caught up in how they are operating instead of why they are in business in the first place. They have built a brand and a house on sand.

Remember: Your unique kingdom calling is so unique to you that it cannot be replaced by anyone else.

Authority: Getting in the Game

The truth of what you believe will be evident by what you do.[36]
BILL POLLARD, AUTHOR, CEO FAIRWYN INVESTMENT COMPANY

Now that you are aware of the false self, have dismantled lies, and shame, and discovered your true identity in God, it's time to move into authority. Knowing and living as your true self allow you to take bigger risks with your time, talent, relationships, and money. I've discovered that I can't compare my life to others because that is not how I will be measured by God for what I've done while I'm here. This gives me even more confidence in living as my authentic self and allows me to be bold in making decisions.

There was a season in my life where I was on the verge of living. I wasn't pushing into risk, but neither was I falling backward in retreat. I was stuck, going nowhere. When you're stuck, you create another false idol. It's the idol of self-preservation caused by fear. I've learned that taking action helps us get to the bull's-eye more quickly. You can have all the faith you want, but unless it is used, you won't make traction. God is looking for individuals who love Him and obey His commandments. When you read His words, they are about hearing *and doing*. Worshiping is essential to our relationship with God, and a life of action is the biggest act of worship unto Him. I believe that living out your own authentic story is the greatest praise to Him. How will your story end? Is your life a battle to fight and a cause worth dying for? Does your heart yearn for the adventure in story and creativity? When thinking about your future, does your heart look forward to what's around the corner, or is it paralyzed by the unknown?

Our calling gives us insight into our identity and the kinds of activities that we are going to be drawn to. Christ knew His calling, which caused Him to lead in authority concerning His mission, which also defined *how* He spent time and *who* He spent time with. This is what I call moving into authority leadership. When you begin to know your mission, you become proactive, not allowing life to simply happen around you. You create boundaries to keep wasteful and empty things out of your life and actively pursue the things that you feel called into. Living this lifestyle isn't for the faint of heart; it requires moving in faith. When faith is present, two things will usually be evident: risk and danger. I spent a majority of my life on the sidelines as a poser. I was suited up, looking like a player, but I didn't have a position or an assignment. I just wanted everyone to believe I would take a hit or give one. I judged myself by my intentions. My challenge to you is to ask yourself if you feel like you're risking much. Are you living in faith? Are you putting yourself out there to be used by God as He wired you?

Getting in the game, in my opinion, means becoming a fearhunter and hunting down those beliefs and habits that rob us of our true identity. I am encouraging you to put on the uniform, accept the assignment, and find out the unique assignment that God has wired you for.

DISCOVER YOUR CALLING AND OWN THE BRAND OF YOU

Career is what you are paid to do; calling is what you are made to do.

BOB SHANK

Simply put, your calling is to fulfill the unique role that only you can fill. I often talk with folks who are open about their life's passions and pursuits, but rarely do I find a person who can say with complete conviction that they know their calling. I believe each one of us is absolutely here on purpose and has a specific calling. Your calling can be found where your potential collides with your passions. The best way to know if you are operating in your calling is to ask, "Can anyone else in the world do what I am doing right now?" If the answer is yes, then I encourage you to look further into opportunities that allow you to be the unique version of you.

Discovering your calling is daunting to most people because the journey itself is overwhelming and uncomfortable. That's what the previous sections were about: the discovery process. Self-discovery terrifies most people because they are afraid of what they might uncover. To me, it is the greatest gateway to freedom because it opens you to move into that sweet spot of authentic living on the other side.

Two years after Chantel and I bought our first home, she became pregnant with our daughter, Griffin. I was presented with the opportunity to join a mentorship with my now mentor, Bob Shank. I declined due to the lack of finances and because I felt it wasn't what I needed. It was exactly what I needed, but I just couldn't see it. We spent the next three years acquiring debt and making investments that were based on superficial desires, which got us tangled up in a huge knot. I finally had enough of a life that was self-absorbed and surrendered myself to following some great leaders who had their lives together. This mentorship turned our lives upside down in a great way.

One day, when I was in a session with my mentor, I told him that I just wanted my calling written on a piece of paper so that I could go out and live it. I wanted so badly to live my life on purpose, knowing how short life is and how fast this life was going by. There was a pressing urgency to finding and pursuing what I was supposed to be doing. Do you ever feel this? I felt like I was simply existing, not thriving and being the true me. I felt like I was doing art for the sake of money, which provided for my family, but I didn't feel truly alive.

The honest truth about discovering calling is that it isn't a solo mission. I discovered more about myself when I started living life with mentors speaking into my life. I realized that I had nothing to measure my life against and no sense of peace when I was journeying alone. Being a fearhunter and gaining techniques for removing fear and shame became most effective when truth was being spoken into my soul on a weekly or monthly basis by my mentors.

Think of your unique style and calling as if you were your own personal brand. This requires a team, a board of advisors, and those who will question and illuminate your blind spots and hidden value in your life. It is crucial to make sure that the people you surround yourself with are sound, trustworthy, and wise. You don't just need friends but serious mentors with whom you can confidently confide in and share your life strategy and mission. I personally have three to five mentors at a time along with a small handful of trusted team members with whom I do life daily.

There is always the risk that some of these mentoring relationships could turn sour. Those whom you thought you could trust may end up no longer on your team. This is to be expected. As seasons change in life, assignments morph into new areas, and you will be required to reassess who's helpful and who's hindering. This will require intention on your part as a brand owner to look critically at the relationships in your life.

Take the issue of mentors seriously in your life. They can buy you time, save you a ton of money, and get you to your sweet spot quicker. Mentorship excites me because life isn't meant to be run as a solo mission. The greatest leaders I have ever met have a board of advisors and a trusted team speaking into their live daily.

ACTION STEP: FIND A MENTOR.

Show me a successful individual and I'll show you someone who had real positive influences in his or her life. I don't care what you do for a living—if you do it well I'm sure there was someone cheering you on or showing the way. A mentor.[37]

DENZEL WASHINGTON, ACTOR

The delicate balance of mentoring someone is not creating them in your own image, but giving them the opportunity to create themselves.[38]

STEVEN SPIELBERG, DIRECTOR, PRODUCER, SCREENWRITER

INTERFERENCE

The duty of cultivating our own personal brand and calling will require ten times more effort than our career ever did. No one else can own your calling, and no one else will put in the hours and dedicate the passion to developing it the way that you will. I can tell you from personal experience that following my calling required facing and eliminating fears that I would never have imagined, especially on the relationship front. I have never received more opposition and interference than when I moved into my calling. Let me tell you, it is the hardest thing I've ever encountered.

Remember that the closer you move toward your authentic self, the more interference you will experience. There are very few individuals who are moving in life at the pace that I am going and desire to go. Many find that my pace is too fast, too intense, or too intentional. The more I dig to discover who I truly am, the more interference I receive from those around me. Everyone wants me to slow down, pull back, and settle in. When you break free from the status quo, your life kicks into a hyperdrive of authentic living. I've been criticized, hated on social media, received threats, and lost relationships while pursuing my calling. Is it worth it? This path can often be lonely, but I am constantly reminded that I am playing for an audience of one. My ultimate customer is God, the one who gave me the time, talent, and treasure to make the most of. I want to encourage you to embrace the fact that the resistance you may experience is simply part of this journey—you are not alone even if you feel like it sometimes.

Here's what I know about fear hunting when it comes to my calling and true self: calling will require you to accept that you will experience resistance. It's guaranteed. Most leaders feel that if there is resistance, they have taken a wrong step. Shame wants you to believe that it's not something you've done wrong, but that there is something wrong with you. If you anticipate this type of resistance, then you will know how to best remove these lies and false identities. Leadership isn't a clean business. Calling requires failure and risk. It's worth it because neither the measurement of your value nor your most important customer is earthly. The standard is a heavenly one, and there is unconditional love and acceptance even when we fail.

Many believers get tripped up when interference happens, and I am no exception. If bad things happen, I assume that I did something wrong; yet this is not always true. Ask yourself, is this resistance condemning or convicting? Condemning often results in feeling bad for no reason, that your value as a human is challenged; you feel discouraged or dirty. This is the enemy. If it's convicting, it will refine some area of life in order to make you stronger, cleaner, braver, and wiser. This is the Lord pruning your life, often to groom you for greater authority and an expansion of territory. This process can be uncomfortable, but embracing the refining of God is where growth comes from. I believe it's time for an audit of your life if you aren't facing resistance in any areas of life. Advancing and claiming new territory usually come with some form of resistance.

So if you are getting pelted with arrows and interference, congrats! You are likely fighting the right battles. Living your calling and partnering with God are the hardest things you'll ever do. However, you can live with certainty that you are living the right life. Why is there interference? Because the things we are discussing here are often countercultural, and you are going against the flow. There is also a struggle because we are living behind enemy lines. The worldview, through God's lens, is contrary to what the culture promotes and advertises. The Bible offers reward *there* (eternity) but most folks want gratification and reward *here*.

God is offering eternal treasure. This is something that cannot be offered anywhere else. Therefore, based on the section we have just covered, is it any wonder we receive so much interference and resistance as we move into our calling? It's tough, but God's glory is illuminated that much more by the overcomer. Resistance is expected. Don't be surprised. Be more concerned if you never experience resistance.

Do not store up for yourselves treasures on earth, where moth and rust destroy, and where thieves break in and steal. But store up for yourselves treasures in heaven, where moth and rust do not destroy, and where thieves do not break in and steal.

JESUS OF NAZARETH (MATTHEW 6:19–20, BSB)

For where your treasure is, there your heart will be also.

JESUS OF NAZARETH (LUKE 12:34, NIV)

#HUNTING TARGETS:

1. Where in your life do you see yourself stepping into healthy risks?

2. For you personally, who are your examples of risk takers and those who live by faith?

3. What is your unique superhero power? (Hint: If some-one said, "Hey invite [enter your name] because he or she brings [fill in your superpower] to the situation," then this will be your passion, your unique skill set, and talent. Example, you might be extremely passionate about childcare, shipping and receiving, accounting, music, management, etc.).

4. What do you love so much that you would do it for free?

5. Where do you feel tired keeping up appearances? How are you being fake and a poser?

6. What image of you elicits embarrassment because of how people might see and experience the new you?

7. What do you fear will happen if you live the authentic you? Loss of friends? Loss of something? Will gaining authenticity and living your heart outweigh the loss of false identities and friends?

8. In what areas of your life do you feel you are on a hamster wheel? Where is all the energy going while the spinning wheel stays in the same spot?

9. What parts of your character make you sick? Is it lack of discipline? Unhealthy habits?

10. In what areas of your life do you feel the most confident and the most authoritative?

11. Rate yourself on a scale of 1-10, with 10 being best, how you feel you are doing in the following areas: Spiritual? Physical? Marital? Parenting? Friends? Giving? Influence? Then write out what you feel is needed to help move the rating up two points.

12. Do you have a mentor and community to help you through life? Who can you meet with locally on a weekly or biweekly basis for accountability and collaboration? If you are alone and would like to join others and me, I created www.masters.life to provide resources and strategies for your life.

#CHAPTER 19

RESPONDING WITH GRATITUDE

The purpose of human life is to serve, and to show compassion and the will to help others.[39]

ALBERT SCHWEITZER, FRENCH THEOLOGIAN

Death is highly motivating for me because it is a constant reminder of the beginning of forever.

NOAH

I WROTE THIS BOOK TO HELP YOU ELIMINATE FEAR AND shame from your life and to reveal the best version of you after this process has taken its course. Uncovering your true identity, your unique assignment, and your irreplaceable calling is the greatest life work you can do! This is also the very best lifestyle you could ever say yes to, especially when you know what the target and rewards are. That said, I urge you to take the time to build a life on the disciplines I have presented. By taking inventory, you will discover that life becomes simplified in how you carry out your calling while living behind enemy lines. As kingdom citizens, we are only on earth for a short time, simply passing through. It is guaranteed that there will be interference, distraction, confusion, and counterfeits. When you leave the pack and head into leadership, you will get pelted first.

Freedom isn't purely the end goal or leaving behind fear and shame; this new freedom invites you to carry out the Lord's vision and help build His kingdom while here on earth with the time you have remaining. Many are called, but few say yes—not just yes to the invitation to know Him, but also to the invitation to join Him in His mission and work.

TRUE PAYBACK

I've been on this earth for almost forty-five years. As I take inventory of my life with counselors, I realize that my life has been one traumatic event after another. It's amazing how I discounted these events as simply regular things that you can expect to encounter as a human. In some cases, I chose chaotic relationships that required me to dismantle the ensuing destruction that occurred. Most cases involved unexpected craziness with family, career, and relationships that I didn't think would have negative results. Through these events, I have learned that in this life, wisdom is the most priceless asset (along with time) that you can possess. You can learn new ways to hack life and save time, but wisdom is the one thing you need to acquire as much of, and as soon as possible. How do we get wisdom? Wisdom is knowledge that has been put into action. You can either experience it or you can get it from others who have cultivated it themselves—aka mentors. Mentors are the ultimate life hack because we can learn through their experiences without having to go through the same trauma.

As I studied King Solomon, one of the wisest men who has ever lived, it became evident that possessions and riches aren't necessarily an outcome of a life well lived. I believe that the whole purpose of redemption is to invite His beloved children into greatness. Why settle for good when great is available? Most Christ followers are so wrapped up in guilt and fear that theirs is a life of gloom and doom; they believe that God is a wrathful God, and their only goal in life is to simply stay out of trouble. Well, there is great news. Our heavenly Father redeemed us so that we can take part in feasting at His table of love and blessing if we are willing to receive it. It is one thing to believe, yet it is another to live that belief in all areas of your life.

WHAT WILL YOU BE DOING 1,000 YEARS FROM NOW?

Sadly, many people accept Jesus as their Savior and then their only goal in life is to try to avoid sinning until they die. They wait patiently to enter a paradise where there is no suffering and pain and believe that their mission is to endure the suffering and pain while on earth and simply look to survive this life. This is the mindset I was taught as I grew up.

The great news for those who have come to know God is that we now have a unique mission that is fueled and supported by the Holy Spirit to carry us through life. We are equipped with spiritual gifts and born with specific traits that are absolutely unique to each of us in order to fulfill our mission. By using what we've been given to honor and build God's kingdom, Scripture teaches that we are storing treasures in heaven that God may reward us accordingly. Before we met Christ, we were not of His business or agenda, nor did we care, and our treasures were stored on earth, subject to decay. Once we met, believed, and started following Him, we surrendered our lives to His will. Unfortunately, many believers treat God like a heavenly bellboy who is here to fulfill our requests rather than seek out the mission that He has for us. What is at the very core of His agenda? Relationships—both for our life here as well as for our eternal destiny.

Understanding the true nature of the love of God causes a deep sense of gratitude toward Him. This is often described as worship, a reverence, and adoration toward God. I believe that a mature sense of worship results in a life lived in earnest toward Him. As the truth of God's love permeated my heart, I became aggressive on hunting fears, shame, and guilt in my life; I wanted it gone ASAP. I dissolved toxic relationships. I drastically filtered new clients and partnerships that I took on. I made spending quality time with my wife and children the paramount priority in my life, and I viewed my career, now my second priority, as a mechanism to bring people into the truth of God's love. I began a vigorous audit of my time, talent, and treasure, measuring how all of these resources were used. I just wish someone would have expressed the truth of God's love and purpose for our lives when I was 15.

Scripture indicates that there will be some form of treasure, rank, and work in heaven (just as when Eden was still perfect, there was work to be done in the garden, and it was a joy for man to work alongside God). When talking to the disciples, Christ let them know that they could be great in His kingdom. What does it take to be great in God's kingdom? In principle, it's actually quite simple because He told us: love God, love people and make disciples. My job in this life is to discover the unique way that I am called to do that.

> *So take the bag of gold from him and give it to the one who has ten bags. For whoever has will be given more, and they will have an abundance. Whoever does not have, even what they have will be taken from them. And throw that worthless servant outside, into the darkness, where there will be weeping and gnashing of teeth.*
>
> JESUS OF NAZARETH (MATTHEW 25:28-30, NIV)

> *You did not choose me, but I chose you and appointed you so that you might go and bear fruit—fruit that will last—and so that whatever you ask in my name the Father will give you.*
>
> JESUS OF NAZARETH (JOHN 15:16, NIV)

GOD'S OBJECTIVE

It's difficult for us to discover God's objective if we're tangled up in the affairs of this world and absorbed in managing sin and false identities. I have seen very few break from the pack of managing sin and into the freedom of fully being on the Lord's agenda. Even though I will still sin and continue to repent and ask for forgiveness to keep moving forward, I don't let the sinner title define me. My natural inclination is sinful because I am human, but it is my supernatural identity and objective to run the race God has set before me. This is even more profound as we take into consideration that the race we run here will determine our heavenly outcome. We will reap the treasures in heaven that we stored while we here on earth.

God's main objective is people. When you stand before your heavenly Father, He will ask, "What did you do with what I gave you?" That question haunts me in the best way every minute of each day, and death is highly motivating for me because it is a constant reminder of the beginning of forever. When He asks me this question, He will look over His shoulder for the people who are standing in heaven as a result of my life. These principles rocked my world so much that it made hunting fears and shame my top priority in order to eliminate the trappings of my false self and live out my true life in His Spirit. This clarifies my life's purpose and causes me to evaluate where I allocate my life's resources (time, effort, money) if I'm to truly live my life for Him.

If our calling is to love Him, love people, and make disciples, how do we actually live this out? I discovered that if I give someone something to eat, somewhere to sleep, or build them a house, I am living out the exhortation in Titus to devote myself "to good works, so as to help in cases of urgent need, and not be unfruitful" (Titus 3:14, ESV). In Romans 10:14, Paul also exhorts us to share the good news of Jesus, stating, "How then will they call on him in whom they have not believed? And how are they to believe in him of whom they have never heard? And how are they to hear without someone preaching?" (ESV). We are called to fill people's hearts with Christ's love while also feeding their stomachs and caring for their practical needs. When I am asked to sign up for charities and giving opportunities, I always make sure they are fulfilling these initiatives that are the highest on my Father's agenda.

> *No soldier in active service entangles himself in the affairs of everyday life, so that he may please the one who enlisted him as a soldier.*
>
> PAUL THE APOSTLE (2 TIMOTHY 2:4)

Let's talk about the story of the rich fool. Jesus told a parable of a man whose land yielded an abundant crop. The man thought to himself that he would build new barns, save up his grain, and take it easy for a few years since he had everything taken care of. But God said to him, "You fool! Even tonight your very life will be taken from you! Then who will get what you have prepared for yourself?" (see Luke 12:20). This man assumed that he was going to live a long life. Little did he know that very night that he would be taken from this world. I also assumed this very thing for many years of my life. I believed I would be around forever and that what I did really didn't matter because I had plenty

RESPONDING WITH GRATITUDE

of life ahead of me. I treated my salvation like a Willy Wonka ticket: I was in the clear because I was "going." However, life takes on a whole new dynamic when you find out the meaning of your life and why He specifically put you here in terms of your calling.

I get occasional pushback from people who say that these principles of stewardship and giving add additional duty and guilt to our grace-based walk with God, and that being fully self-sufficient, He doesn't need anything from us. I cannot stress enough that these principles are not out of duty, but out of love and gratitude for who He is and what He has provided for us. Scripture tells us that God's entire agenda for our lives is to bear fruit; this principle is well illustrated by Paul in his letter to the Philippians. Paul had asked the Philippian church to give to other churches due to their various needs, stating, "not that I seek the gift, but I seek the fruit that increases to your credit" (Philippian 4:17, ESV). Paul makes it clear that their giving caused their lives to be fruitful and further stated that it was "a fragrant offering, a sacrifice acceptable and pleasing to God" (verse 18). The Philippian church had blessed Paul, their brethren in need, God, and *additionally* the language used indicates that their act of love was *credited* to their heavenly account. This lovely example shows us the exponential growth that God has in mind for our intentional acts of love.

I'll quote Pollard again: "The truth of what you believe will be evident by what you do."[40]

Our mission in life is to partner with God to determine how our lives can bear the most fruit and to also determine who we partner with on this journey. The fruitfulness of my decisions with Chantel and the kids, my career, and each one of my relationships will all be measured at the end of my life. The Lord's desire is that we would discover the secrets of kingdom stewardship because what we do here matters more than we see in our physical realm. Jesus said, "A new commandment I give to you, that you love one another, even as I have loved you" (John 13:34), and His Word instructs us to obey His commands, which means that our faith should manifest itself in action.

At this point, you might feel like you have been on an emotional roller coaster. You may feel like you will want to dismantle everything in your life because you have discovered the secret of the kingdom. You will be a true fearhunter because your motive for living will be removing anything that gets in the way of bearing fruit and making a positive impact in the world. The sooner fear and shame are dealt with, the sooner we can focus on building eternal wealth and significance. You will be like the man who discovered the treasure in the field. He buried it and left, sold all that he had to come back and buy the field. Speaking personally, this is exactly what it was like for me.

Once I knew and found out what God wanted and had planned for my family and me, I wanted as much of it as I could possibly get. We started downsizing our life, selling our properties, getting smaller, and hacking life and time every way possible so that we wouldn't owe anything to anyone. We wanted to live in freedom, available to serve our Father and not be entangled by earthly riches and honor, power, and prestige. I was so angry for allowing myself to get tripped up by the culture's pressure to amass wealth and diversify my funds to expand our retirement. These changes were a roller coaster because our hearts knew our actions to be true, yet we still had internal struggles to implement these things, and the culture encouraged us to do everything the opposite.

As you live for eternity, the contrast between yourself and the culture will increase with time, so expect it. The more you live outside the culture, the masses will think you're nuts. Your new life will have you taking risks, not just in facing fear and shame. These challenges will seem small compared to the fear and confrontation of a kingdom initiative that requires you to put your entire life on the line. Leadership in God's kingdom comes at a price, but it's worth it. Are you willing to gain your life by losing what you thought was your life?

Just like I said, His currency and will are paramount. The moment you know, you know. The question is, now that you know, what do you plan to do? You can't plead ignorance at the end of your life. My prayer for you is that you will make a commitment to discover this truth further and act on the wisdom you've been given. If you are a believer and have been for some time, I am asking you to make a proclamation between Him and you. Proclaim that you will make a commitment to answer the call to action of being on His agenda and His currency; that your time, talent, and treasure will be used to increase His kingdom; that you will commit to discovering your unique calling; that you will ask Him to pour out His love and truth onto you through His Word, your friends, and prayer. That is what He did for me and continues to do.

THE ASSIGNMENT GROWING

Here's what is amazing. As your life takes on new dimensions of ridding the fear and shame, you create added capacity to build your new life and identity in carrying out your calling. This is the stage where it gets extremely exciting and fun. The more I worked this process, the more refined my calling became. My best use of time on this planet in my personal life is spending time with my wife and children and building solid relationships that point others to Christ. In terms of my craft, I learned that my greatest use of my time is painting, drawing, writing, and mentoring individuals on these topics. I don't say yes to many things outside of those parameters. I would be doing a disservice to those whom I would be working with if I did so. These boundaries allow me to live in the sweet spot of my calling and work to the best of my abilities.

Now, the secret is to use those areas as avenues to expose people to God's love. Each of these areas are important ways that I serve as I live my life tracking my spiritual portfolio in the same way an investor would diversify his finances. The goal is to stay focused on your strengths and don't take the bait from the enemy and the world to pull you into other less-fitting projects. When you find your sweet spot, it allows you to produce a quality of fruit that would not be produced if you were mediocre at a million things. They might all bear some fruit, but not as much as if you stayed in your sweet spot. If God's children are willing to discipline themselves to steward their life wisely, how does He respond? He gives them more to manage.

I see each of our personal brands as a brand within God's brand—a franchise of His kingdom. Our goal in life is to build and run it as such. When most leaders and so-called successful people make more money, they usually increase their lifestyle. They increase their standard of living instead of their standard of giving. We are meant to live our lives as givers—not just our money, but ourselves as well. Most perceive life as a challenge to amass wealth, hoard as much as possible, build a retirement, and coast their way to death. In contrast, God invites us to take Him up on the offer that He will entrust more to us if we steward His resources wisely. In short, God gets excited when His children go from being controllers to distributors.

As we look at our lives as a brand, I think of us like a winery. We labor to take our lives and yield a crop that will last into eternity—forever paying us a dividend. Most people build a life, but God invites us to build a business where our life is the distribution channel of His product: love, which is a free gift. Our job is to figure out how big of a winery we can build, how much land we can acquire, and how much product we can yield. More importantly, seed that is saved and hoarded will rot. Many believers just want to be comfortable and aren't much different than the general public in that they just want to have a safe and predictable life. Being a believer involves risk; it requires faith and looking beyond the horizon to believe that He will deliver. When the lake starts to fill with blessing, people want to build a dam because they don't believe God will keep sending the rain. He's asking us to break the dam, let His product reach the world through our pipelines, and trust that He will keep sending rain and filling the lake.

ROYALTIES IN HEAVEN

As we have traveled from the beginning of this book until now, we have learned how to dismantle and remove fear and shame all the while looking at the reward we can partake of as a result of creating margins and capacity for God's kingdom. These discoveries excited me a great deal. Life isn't just about becoming spiritually sober but includes the bonus of abundance that our heavenly Father adds over and above the gift of salvation.

There is another gem of wisdom and secret to the kingdom that I learned through my mentor that left me speechless. This nugget alone transformed my entire life and was like adding fuel to the already roaring fire I had burning in my soul.

If you ever have a chance to read *The Law of Rewards*, written by Randy Alcorn, you will discover the paramount message that Christ taught regarding rewards and stewardship. God's Word clearly spells out what will happen if we invest our treasure into those initiatives that increase and build God's kingdom. The passage in Corinthians that we covered earlier discusses the two options of materials that we can build with while on earth. One group is wood, hay, and straw and the other is gold, silver, and costly stones representing an eternal investment that will stand the test of fire. If you invest in worldly possessions and material goods (wood, hay, and straw), they are vulnerable to fire, can be stolen, or they can simply rot or fade away. If you put your investment into an eternal safe, it will pay a valuable return where you will need it most—eternity, where it cannot be damaged. When I stop to think about this, it changes everything. Chantel and I started thinking, "What can we invest in that will last beyond this world and that will pay us the biggest return where we will value it most?" The motivation for wise decision making and getting fears and shame out of the way became even more urgent because not only was this fear hunting about building a successful life to give more, but it also became evident that there could even be a better mechanism for giving.

Look at the life of Paul. Paul was a tentmaker as a business-man, and he spent his life in the workplace traveling around his region meeting with vendors, partners, and various other people. His life impact wasn't a one-time event. If we travel back to Paul's journey, in the beginning, he was a self-righteous man who was persecuting Christians to the point of death. Later in his life, God interrupted him on a walk and blindsided him. Literally. Paul now understood the gravity and reality of God's truth, love, and grace. Paul knew his assignment was now to take this message to the land around him with the time, talent, and money that he had. So what did he do? He made his primary focus of life to not waste any time. Paul realized that he only had so much time. Even more, Paul understood that he wanted to bear as much fruit as possible so that he could reap the benefits of this fruit where it mattered most—eternity. My question for you, friend, is this: Do you realize and believe the truth that God richly rewards those who make their agenda His agenda?

So where do royalties come into play? Well, Paul started writing letters. Paul knew that the way he would be rewarded in heaven was through the relationships he helped point toward Christ and that any intellectual property he invested there would keep reaping rewards without him being present. These letters were God-inspired and became a part of the Bible. What if each time someone reads Paul's words, follows them, and produces fruit, Paul gets a royalty payment in heaven even though he isn't here? (This is what the language Paul used in speaking to the Philippian church demonstrated earlier.) So the question for us is this: Are we stewarding our time, talent, and treasure to create opportunities that will pay dividends in the kingdom for eternity? God invites His children into this reward and encourages us to grab all we can. "Do not store up for yourselves treasures on earth, where moth and rust destroy, and where thieves break in and steal. But store up for yourselves treasures in heaven, where moth and rust do not destroy, and where thieves do not break in and steal" (Matthew 6:19–20, BSB).

Another way to describe this concept is stock. My mentor Bob and I have talked a great deal about what it would be like to compare kingdom stock to Apple stock. What if a representative from Apple made you aware that Apple stock was available to you at twenty-five cents a share? How much would you buy? What action and steps would you take to acquire the stock? How ridiculous would you be willing to be or do in order to get as much as you could? For me, I would go all out and take out as many loans as possible to grab all I could. Well, the return on the Apple stock would be abundant but still nowhere close to the return that our heavenly Father promises in His Word to those who learn the secret of the kingdom and to the return He will give you in eternity forever. Apple stock might pay you well here for a while, but kingdom stock will pay you in eternity. Also, the Lord promises to give us a return on whatever we send ahead. So, if you are able to grasp the paramount importance of stewardship and our Father's agenda, then you, my friend, have cracked the code of "Who am I, why am I here, what am I supposed to do?" And all that's left is to strategically plan to do it.

CREATING A LIFE WHERE YOUR FRUIT GROWS ON OTHER PEOPLE'S TREES

As we've seen in the example of Paul's life, it is evident that stewardship is of ultimate importance to our Father. It has been His design and His agenda since day one. As we grow in our depth of understanding stewardship, we realize that there is a multi-dimensional aspect to it and that our goal is to also grow fruit on other people's trees. What does this mean? This means that we create relationships, investments, and opportunities where fruit will be born without us being there and after we're gone.

When this personally hit my life I had to stop looking at life in two dimensions: family and career. I thought the only way I could give more money was by making more money. This belief is untrue. I began creating intellectual property that would run in the background of my life, bearing fruit in my lifetime and beyond. I started writing books, blogging, filming mentorship videos, and teaching through noahuniversity.com and masters.life. These are avenues that allow the wisdom that was given to me through God's Word and mentors to reach as many people as possible—not just to those in my neighborhood, but to the world. If the Lord's command is to love God, love people and make disciples, then this command means leveraging our lives to impact as many other people as possible. What I'm describing is discipleship/stewardship in hyperdrive. Fear and shame will continue to rob us of the ability to bear fruit and gain rewards if we are in a state of management of fear and sin on a regular basis.

Take caution: It's really easy for leaders who discover these truths to start blasting their machine gun of impact all over the place. A good sign of leadership is restraint. Another way to put it is, we are aiming for quality over quantity. As a leader, the tendency is to desire to impact as many people as possible. In the case of stewardship and discipleship, the key is time. Time has to be hacked. The way I do this is by finding runners. If you've ever been around a multi-level network marketing company, they operate most efficiently by using runners. These are the leaders who take the message or product and go deep with it. It becomes their life and calling.

There can be no better example of this than the ministry of Jesus. He grew in wisdom and in stature for thirty years and then embarked on His ministry, which took three years. Jesus often spoke to multitudes. His message was for mankind and the entire world; however, when He spoke to thousands, He often had just a few who wanted to run the marathon with Him. Jesus looked for twelve, and trust me, they weren't perfect. They were ordinary, everyday people like you and me. Through the twelve, He established the foundation of His kingdom. Many heard the message, but Jesus was looking for runners and those who wanted to bear fruit. The fascinating thing is this: Jesus knew His time was coming to a close. Time was running out; however, He made time for those willing to be discipled. He knew they would run with the gospel and duplicate the discipleship model they had learned. Jesus knew His investment was safe in the lives that ran after He was gone.

As ambassadors, we are looking to reach the world with the good news, and the goal is to find runners who are willing to be mentored and trained and who will also run with the good news and bear fruit as well—this becomes exponential growth. It's challenging as a leader because the more wisdom you gain and people you influence, the more requests you get to lead and mentor. The key is to find those individuals with the most potential for kingdom impact. Jesus spent quality time with leaders that He could groom and shape.

The runners who will come into your life will become evident. Serve the people God puts in your path and help raise their tide for impact. The fruit of your mentors' lives will grow on your tree and your fruit will grow in the others you mentor. This is God's design. Life isn't meant to be lived as a solo mission.

#HUNTING TARGETS

1. What do you want your tombstone to read?

2. What time, talent, and treasure could you create that would expose people to God's love? What activities, movements, or initiatives that are building assets for eternal impact excite you?

3. What areas of your life need to be cut and removed to provide more time to work on initiatives that provide eternal impact and spiritual fruit?

4. On a scale of 1-10, how much do you feel your life is an act of worship to God? What would it take to move that score up two points?

5. Is there enough evidence on your social media and lifestyle that people can tell what you stand for and are about? Do you follow people who are living the lifestyle that you want? What are they doing that you are attracted to?

6. Who in your life do you have an influence on and access to? Where can you step into the risk of being intentional with them? How can you let them know they matter, are loved, and are important?

7. Do you feel you have pursued the relationships in your life with 100 percent authenticity?

8. If your closest friends sat at the dining room table with your spouse and children, what report card would your family give you?

9. If your family is your first ministry, have you forsaken your family in any area for the growth of your influence outside the home?

10. What have you been using in life up to this point as a measuring stick for success? Money? Power? Position?

11. How do you feel about yourself when you understand that God loves you and gives you the gift of grace through sacrificing His Son so that you may have the free gift of eternity? Do you realize how much you matter? How much you are loved? How great a life waits in front of you?

12. Since you are a franchise and a brand inside the kingdom of God, what areas, such as talents and unique gifts, produce the most fruit and impact for you? If you removed 80 percent of all activities and focused on the 20 percent of what you do best, what would be the activities you would do daily? Weekly? Remember, we don't base our value on how much time something takes. We base our value on the revenue, impact, and significance our activity creates. Our aim is to do our favorite work, in the least amount of time, making the most revenue and impact as possible.

13. Everyone needs a mentor. Who is pouring into you, and who are you pouring into? Who in your life can become a part of your bottom line and investment where your fruit and wisdom grow on their tree?

#CHAPTER 20

UNCONDITIONAL SURRENDER

The more often he feels without acting, the less he will be able ever to act, and, in the long run, the less he will be able to feel.[41]

C. S. LEWIS, *THE SCREWTAPE LETTERS*

We are His children and coheirs of His kingdom, destined to live fearlessly, trusting in Him.

NOAH

WE HAVE GONE THROUGH THE FOLLOWING STEPS THUS far:

1. Dismantling the Fake Identity
2. Establishing Your True Identity
3. Moving in Your Authority
4. Living Out Your Calling

In this last chapter, I want to discuss some practical steps that you can start taking immediately!

WHAT'S THE WORST-CASE SCENARIO?

Do you remember the story from chapter 3 where I was driving my car and experienced a barrage of negative self-talk while dreaming about taking a risk with my business? My false self made me question my financial security, my shelter, my creativity, my timing, and almost every relationship I had. Thankfully, I had been practicing my fear hunting at that point, so I fought back. As I continued to drive, I asked myself, "What is the worst-case scenario of going after these dreams of being authentic and true to myself? Let's say nobody buys it. Okay, that's fine. What other people think of me is none of my business. So maybe there is a loss of income. Fine. We have to sell our house and move in with family or significantly downsize. Is that terrible? Would that really be the worst-case scenario?"

I started to realize that the only thing holding me back wasn't money or time. It was simply my way of thinking and the choices I was making. We get to choose the life we want. So we started eliminating everything in our life to reach the life we wanted. We started to trim every bill and every expense. We sold things to get out of debt, which gave us an immediate $3,000 monthly raise. This season was the most terrifying of our lives while also being the most liberating. Each bold move provided freedom and more time. We got rid of properties because they cost us time and money and were a false security. We began homeschooling and had more time to help our special needs' son with his autism.

How did this happen? We *chose* to make it happen. We started with the ideal day and the ideal life we wanted to live. As Stephen Covey said it, we began "with the end in mind."[42] We desired as much time together as possible as a family. We wanted to raise our kids and be the ones showing them how to become leaders and influencers for God's love. We wanted to teach them how to be entrepreneurs and hold the measuring stick of success for themselves. We took life and ran with it. We made work fit our lives, not our lives to fit around our work. This came with some serious growing pains and transitions, but they have been beyond worth it. We didn't even realize just how spent and tapped out we were, leaving no room for fun or freedom, until we chose to make these changes.

One of the smartest things we did was to look for ways to make revenue while not working any harder. We transitioned my teachings into an online program (noahuniversity.com), enabling me to travel less often and allowing me the freedom to be with my family and to paint. As we minimized our lives, we began to look for ways to create more revenue in other business opportunities. Being fearless allowed me to stop asking, "Why?" and start saying, "Why not?" Life then became a portfolio instead of only a dimension of family and career. We removed the ceiling and hindrances of the culture and the workplace, preventing both from defining our identities, and moved into a life of purpose, meaning, and giving. This can't happen when you are paralyzed by fear and shame because you will have one foot tethered to the past, keeping you from your future.

The best-case scenario is often disguised as the worst-case scenario when it comes to our dreams and ideal life. Very few people are willing to travel to unknown places and make decisions that lead into unknown areas of life. Everyone is looking for a guarantee. These days I'm most comfortable exploring ways to hack life by breaking out the machete and hacking away at a new trail. We can settle for the status quo of the familiar, but that is so yesterday. I'd rather fail tremendously than go to bed each night haunted by regret.

A WORD ABOUT FAITH

Your kingdom calling is so specialized to you that it cannot be replaced by anyone else on earth. What you have to offer this world can only be done by you and no one else.

NOAH

While speaking with my mentor about faith, it became evident that a majority of my life didn't require much faith. When we ask folks how they are doing, they might say they are "living by faith." The truth is that a life lived by faith is a life that requires risk and/or danger. Otherwise, faith becomes unnecessary. I realized that my life didn't contain kingdom-based initiatives that required faith. A majority of my life was a rinse and repeat of the same thing over and over just trying to make life more comfortable. My mission was to create a business so that I could make money to provide the nicest life for my family that I could. My aim and target were way off! I had Jesus in my life, but I made Him a heavenly bellboy answering to all my needs and requests based on self-gratification in earthly possessions. The moment I understood the law of rewards and the powerful role I had in kingdom stewardship, everything changed. Life became about being faithful in all areas. His agenda became my agenda and faith kicked in.

What good is it, my brothers and sisters, if someone claims to have faith but has no deeds? Can such faith save them? Suppose a brother or a sister is without clothes and daily food. If one of you says to them, "Go in peace; keep warm and well fed," but does nothing about their physical needs, what good is it? In the same way, faith by itself, if it is not accompanied by action, is dead.

But someone will say, "You have faith; I have deeds." Show me your faith without deeds, and I will show you my faith by my deeds. You believe that there is one God. Good! Even the demons believe that — and shudder.

You foolish person, do you want evidence that faith without deeds is useless? Was not our father Abraham considered righteous for what he did when he offered his son Isaac on the altar? You see that his faith and his actions were working together, and his faith was made complete by what he did. And the scripture was fulfilled that says, "Abraham believed God, and it was credited to

*him as righteousness," and he was called God's friend.
You see that a person is considered righteous by what they
do and not by faith alone.*

*In the same way, was not even Rahab the prostitute
considered righteous for what she did when she gave
lodging to the spies and sent them off in a different
direction? As the body without the spirit is dead, so faith
without deeds is dead.*

JAMES 2:14–26 (NIV)

JUST SAY YES

*No one is more excited about your life and calling
than He is.*

NOAH

As you wrap up this book, you might be angry or frustrated because you feel obligated to do something more. Anger, frustration, and other emotions provide road maps of your heart and point to the condition of your spirit. You might be cooked, done, well-done, and cinnamon toast crunch with your life up until now. That's okay, take a deep breath and exhale. A life run on self-will can be exhausting even for a person who has a relationship with God. Guessing your way through life is hard work and can cause spiritual burnout.

Many churches don't speak into stewardship or discuss the development of your personal calling. Maybe you've been looking and needing something more but didn't understand what the missing components were. I have also struggled with finding my path, searching everywhere for biblical leadership mentoring that would help me discover my calling from those who had already cracked the code of kingdom stewardship, yet I couldn't find it. What I found was that saying yes to the assignment wasn't as hard as it seemed, though it did require faith and courage to act on the truth. The Lord is looking for those willing to answer the call. He promises rewards, knowing the invitation is for many but few actually say yes.

> *For many are called, but few are chosen.*
>
> JESUS OF NAZARETH (MATTHEW 22:14, NLT)

Having these truths and knowledge, but not acting on them, isn't saying yes. It is essentially saying no. Our mission is to find our assignment, our calling, and our unique design in His mission. By doing so, we become a distributor of His assets—faith, hope, love, and eternal life. If I am going to be in any business, it is going to be God's business. As James, the brother of Jesus, so eloquently put it:

> *Do not merely listen to the word, and so deceive yourselves.*
> *Do what it says. Anyone who listens to the word but*
> *does not do what it says is like someone who looks at his*
> *face in a mirror and, after looking at himself, goes away*
> *and immediately forgets what he looks like. But whoever*
> *looks intently into the perfect law that gives freedom, and*
> *continues in it—not forgetting what they have heard, but*
> *doing it—they will be blessed in what they do.*
>
> JAMES, THE BROTHER OF JESUS (JAMES 1:22–25, NIV)

We all share the same calling: love God, love people, and make disciples. Our God-given goal is to find out how we each do that based on our unique abilities, talents, and gifts. Your kingdom calling is so specialized to you that it cannot be replaced by anyone else on earth. What you have to offer this world can only be done by you and no one else. My prayer for you is that you continue to hunt the fears you have made agreements with that have become evident in your life. Fear is the enemy of faith and the gateway between us and the life we are destined to live. We have to get on the offense, hunting and removing fear and shame. If we don't, our lives will be spent in management, our calling will remain inactive, and our life won't be purposeful.

Jesus said, "I came that they may have life, and have it abundantly" (John 10:10) This abundance isn't only reserved for when we get to heaven. It is also meant to be experienced while we are here on earth. We are His children and coheirs of His kingdom, destined to live fearlessly, trusting in Him.

For God has not given us a spirit of fear and timidity, but of power, love, and self-discipline.

PAUL THE APOSTLE (2 TIMOTHY 1:7, NLT)

You have what it takes. You have several tools to remove shame and fear. You have the framework to design a life based on His purposes. The ability to make choices is a beautiful gift from God. My question for you is, will you grab your gear, take your unique personality and passions, and set out into your life of abundance? While on this journey of risk and danger, will you become a fearhunter, proactively living on the offense? Your life is waiting to happen. Are you going to happen to life? Or is life going to happen to you?

Your heavenly Father created you. You are His masterpiece clothed in righteousness. He will never give you an assignment without the resources or provision to carry it out. This life requires assembly with you and with Him. It's a partnership—a relationship. No one is more excited about your life and calling than He is. He wants to walk the journey with you as you discover it. God is always pursuing your heart, even when you are not pursuing His. Even while you sleep, He watches over you and prays for you. He's extremely excited to be with you in the moment-by-moment process of life.

You get to choose how you will live this life. You can either base your worth on your past record of shame and fear or embrace the truth that God doesn't care where you've been. He's excited about who you are becoming and where you are headed. The new life and vehicle that God wants you to drive does not have a rearview mirror.

I'm in your corner.

#NOTES

1. C. S. Lewis, *The Screwtape Letters* (HarperOne, 2015).
2. Justin Stomvall, "The Hidden Truth Behind Manhood–Finding freedom from our hiddenness," justinstumvoll.com/the-hidden-truth-behind-manhood-finding-freedom-from-our-hiddenness.
3. Marianne Williamsson, *Return to Love: Reflections on the Principles of a Course in Miracles* (HarperCollins, 1992).
4. Demi Moore quoting someone who wrote to her, *The Mirror*, www.mirror.co.uk/3am/celebrity-news/demi-moore-fears-shes-not-157206.
5. Kathie Lee Gifford, *Parade*, parade.com/498992/sks14c/happy-birthday-kathie-lee-gifford-15-of-her-most-inspiring-quotes.
6. Naveen Jain, *Huffpost*, "Dear CEOs, Celebrate Failure," www.huffingtonpost.com/naveen-jain/dont-be-a-tiger-mom-ceo-c_b_835623.html.
7. Denis Waitley, izquotes.com/quote/354755.
8. Debbie Ford, *Why Good People Do Bad Things: How to Stop Being Your Own Worst Enemy* (HarperOne, 2009).

9. Tad Williams, www.tadwilliams.com/vault/quotes.

10. Chris Pine, Business Insider, "8 highly successful celebrities share their most valuable piece of career advice," www.businessinsider.in/entertainment/people/8-highly-successful-celebrities-share-their-most-valuable-piece-of-career-advice/slidelist/51503025.cms.

11. Twyla Tharp, www.achievement.org/achiever/twyla-tharp.

12. Steve Jobs, from his speech given at Stanford University in 2005, *The Guardian*, https://www.theguardian.com/technology/2011/oct/06/steve-jobs-pancreas-cancer.

13. Joyce Meyer, *The Power of Being Positive: Enjoying God Forever* (FaithWords, 2003).

14. Marilyn Manson, *Brainy Quote*, www.brainyquote.com/quotes/marilyn_manson_192760.

15. Alan Kay, en.wikiquote.org/wiki/Alan_Kay.

16. Will Smith, www.imdb.com/title/tt1815862/quotes.

17. Jack Canfield, Mark Hansen, Les Hewitt, *The Power of Focus* (Vintage/Ebury, a Division of Random, 2001).

18. Bryan Cranston, *Brainy Quote*, www.brainyquote.com/quotes/bryan_cranston_491025.

19. Henri Nouwen, *A Cry for Mercy: Prayers from the Genesee* (Image, 2002).

20. Paul Valéry, *Brainy Quote,* www.brainyquote.com/quotes/paul_valery_104279.

21. Dr. Wayne Dyer, "The Ego Illusion," www.drwaynedyer.com/blog/the-ego-illusion.

22. Tim Ferriss, www.azquotes.com/quote/730822.

23. Moliere,*Brainy Quote*, www.brainyquote.com/quotes/moliere_382611.

24. Maya Angelou, *Huffpost*, "The 3 Lessons Maya Angelou Taught Us About Coping," www.huffingtonpost.com/mequilibrium/maya-angelou-legacy_b_5479355.html.

25. Arnold Schwarzenegger, *Brainy Quote*, www.brainyquote.com/quotes/arnold_schwarzenegger_116694.

26. Paul J. Meyer, *Brainy Quote*, www.brainyquote.com/quotes/paul_j_meyer_135516.
27. Colin Powell, *Brainy Quote*, www.brainyquote.com/quotes/colin_powell_119271.
28. Oswald Chambers, *My Utmost for His Highest*, January 14, utmost.org/called-by-god.
29. Erin Hanson, *Huffpost*, www.huffingtonpost.com/entry/why-fall-when-you-can-fly_us_5853e009e4b06ae7ec2a3d7b.
30. Morihei Ueshiba, *Brainy Quote*, www.brainyquote.com/quotes/morihei_ueshiba_183597.
31. Jack Canfield, *Huffpost*, www.huffingtonpost.co.uk/pam-warren/we-need-purpose-and-to-kn_b_12194952.html.
32. Thomas Kinkade, *Brainy Quote*, www.brainyquote.com/quotes/thomas_kinkade_552484.
33. Barbara De Angelis, *Are You the One for Me?: Knowing Who's Right and Avoiding Who's Wrong* (Dell, 1993).
34. Lance Secretan, *The Spark, the Flame, and the Torch* (The Secretan Center Inc., 2010).
35. Simon Mainwaring, www.wefirstbranding.com/brands/why-brands-that-do-good-must-also-do-it-well.
36. Bill Pollard, source unknown.
37. Denzel Washington, *Guideposts*, www.guideposts.org/better-living/positive-living/the-mentors-hell-never-forget.
38. Steven Spielberg, www.theinvisiblementor.com/mentoring-quotes-national-mentoring-month.
39. Albert Schweitzer, en.wikiquote.org/wiki/Talk:Albert_Schweitzer.
40. Bill Pollard, source unknown.
41. C. S. Lewis, *The Screwtape Letters* (HarperOne, 2015).
42. Stephen Covey, www.stephencovey.com/7habits/7habits-habit2.php.

More resources and materials are available
that I would love for you to check out.

Visit me at www.noahuniversity.com
and www.masters.life.

ADDITIONAL ACKNOWLEDGMENTS

Thanks to Justin Stumvoll for your guidance through the mental prisons and nightmares. Laura Duncan for your guidance and illumination of the process and healing. Abi Stumvoll for reminding me how our Father sees me. Thanks to Jenn Ripley for your contribution and helping keep the message of the Lord's heart intact throughout this project. Thanks to Ryan Sprenger for your support and contribution. Thanks to Justis Earle for your input and touch, making this project all it can be. Thank you to Jason Borneman, Ian Utile, and Dave Michael for your continued, unconditional support. Thanks to Jared Andreasen for your incredible loyalty, dedication, and support.

31 DISCIPLINES OF HIGHLY SUCCESSFUL CREATIVE ENTREPRENEURS

A DAILY DOSE OF INSPIRATION TO SHARPEN YOUR CREATIVE EDGE

Do you find yourself generating innovative ideas and incredible dreams but lacking the disciplines and strategies to bring them to life?

With over 30 years of creative experience under his belt, Noah Elias has developed 31 daily devotionals to encourage the development of healthy practices and habits to better steward your time, talent, money, and relationships.

This book lays out simple yet comprehensive strategies for living life with purpose. It will enable you to rise to a level of creativity and output that few entrepreneurs possess!

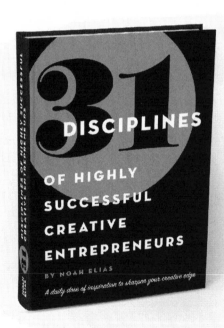

AVAILABLE NOW!
VISIT NOAHFINEART.COM

ABOUT THE AUTHOR

The story for this Orange County native began humbly, selling art door to door as a teenager on a bicycle. At just 16, Noah was handing out business cards to create custom art, signs, and illustrations for local businesses.

Driven to succeed, young Noah's career began to take off as large corporations and celebrities began to notice his talent. Noah has produced paintings for Lexus Motorcars, Toyota, Levi Strauss, Nordstrom, CBS Television, and Fox TV. Noah's celebrity work started with Craig T. Nelson and others such as Val Kilmer, Barbra Streisand, Ted Danson, and Tom Cruise.

Noah's work elevated globally when he was featured on The Learning Channel's show *Rides,* and Universal Studios sought Noah's expertise in designing Suki's sports car in *2 Fast 2 Furious.* His career elevated again when MTV commissioned Noah to create pieces for the hit TV show, *Rob and Big,* and also featured his work on episodes of *Meet the Barkers* with Travis Barker, a friend and collector of Noah's work. Noah formed relationships with such brands as Carey Hart of "Hart and Huntington," who features his work in various tattoo shops, and he has also designed the tattoos on recording artist Pink for one of her music videos.

One of Noah's favorite and most fruitful partnerships has been with The Walt Disney Company™ where he created a line of "Noah" versions of the characters. These have become a huge favorite among Disney collectors and fans worldwide. His creations are featured on all Disney Cruise Line Ships, at Walt Disney World in Orlando, Florida, and Disneyland Resort in Anaheim, California.

Noah believes that "success is not judged by status, power, or prestige, but rather the lives impacted for God's glory." He intentionally seeks to empower other creatives through his mentoring site: NoahUniversity.com. All aspects of Noah's work are available at NoahFineArt.com.

Noah still happily resides in Orange County with his wife, Chantel, and two children, Noah and Griffin.